Praise for Lean UX

"The quality of the user experience has become the most important differentiator for a company's product. In Lean UX, Josh Seiden and Jeff Gothelf highlight the methods and strategies for ensuring that great experiences are built with as little waste as possible in a collaborative, cross-functional effort. It is a must read not just for designers, but for everyone on the team from executive leadership to intern."

Tom Boates—Founder/CEO of Brilliant

"If you're struggling to ship winning user experiences with agile development methods, get this book! Jeff and Josh share proven methods for creative ideation, planning, and problem-solving without heavy deliverable baggage. The new edition brings some crucial updates, including help with designing and tracking experiments, and refinements to many of the critical tools of lean UX."

Christian Crumlish—VP Product, 7cups.com; Coauthor of
***Designing Social Interfaces*, Second Edition**

"In the time since Lean UX was first published, the practices it outlines have become widespread. The revised and expanded Lean UX 2nd Edition will show you how to apply Lean UX thinking to both green fields and sustaining innovation projects, create the right company culture for success and inspire you with new case studies of Lean UX in practice."

Lane Goldstone—Cofounder Brooklyn Copper Cookware

"Jeff and Josh's passion for getting UX (and really all of product development) right comes across powerfully in this detailed yet eminently readable book. The case studies, examples, and research serve to highlight the power of building a Lean UX process, and there's a great deal of actionable advice taken from these. I'm ordering a copy for everyone on our design, UX, and product teams at Moz."

Rand Fishkin—CEO and Cofounder, Moz

"A fantastic combination of case studies and practical advice that your team can use today. Whether you're at a startup or a Fortune 500 company, this book will change the way you build products."

Laura Klein—Author of *UX for Lean Startups*

"Lean UX provides a prescriptive framework for how to build better products, moving design away from pixel perfection for the sake of it, toward iterative learning, smarter effort, and outcome-based results. Product managers, business owners, and startup employees—along with designers—can benefit greatly from Lean UX."

Ben Yoskovitz—Founding Partner, Highline BETA

SECOND EDITION

Lean UX

Designing Great Products with Agile Teams

Jeff Gothelf and Josh Seiden

Beijing · Boston · Farnham · Sebastopol · Tokyo

Lean UX

by Jeff Gothelf and Josh Seiden

Copyright © 2016 Jeff Gothelf and Josh Seiden. All rights reserved.

Printed in the United States of America.

Published by O'Reilly Media, Inc., 1005 Gravenstein Highway North, Sebastopol, CA 95472.

O'Reilly books may be purchased for educational, business, or sales promotional use. Online editions are also available for most titles (*http://oreilly.com/safari*). For more information, contact our corporate/institutional sales department: 800-998-9938 or *corporate@oreilly.com*.

Development Editor: Angela Rufino	**Indexer:** Ellen Troutman-Zaig
Acquisitions Editor: Nicolas Lombardi	**Interior Designer:** David Futato
Production Editor: Colleen Cole	**Cover Designer:** Karen Montgomery
Copyeditor: Octal Publishing, Inc.	**Illustrator:** Rebecca Demarest
Proofreader: Kim Cofer	

March 2013:	First Edition
September 2016:	Second Edition

Revision History for the Second Edition

2016-09-09:	First Release
2016-11-18:	Second Release
2017-02-03:	Third Release
2017-06-23:	Fourth Release

See *http://oreilly.com/catalog/errata.csp?isbn=9781491953600* for release details.

The O'Reilly logo is a registered trademark of O'Reilly Media, Inc. *Lean UX*, the cover image, and related trade dress are trademarks of O'Reilly Media, Inc.

While the publisher and the authors have used good faith efforts to ensure that the information and instructions contained in this work are accurate, the publisher and the authors disclaim all responsibility for errors or omissions, including without limitation responsibility for damages resulting from the use of or reliance on this work. Use of the information and instructions contained in this work is at your own risk. If any code samples or other technology this work contains or describes is subject to open source licenses or the intellectual property rights of others, it is your responsibility to ensure that your use thereof complies with such licenses and/or rights.

978-1-491-95360-0

[LSCC]

For Carrie, Grace, and Sophie

...and Vicky, Naomi, Amanda, and Joey.

Contents

Foreword.. XI

Authors' Note... XV

Preface.. XIX

PART I: INTRODUCTION AND PRINCIPLES

Chapter 1
Lean UX: More Important Now Than Ever Before 3

Chapter 2
Principles 7

PART II: PROCESS

Chapter 3
Driving Vision with Outcomes 21

Chapter 4
Collaborative Design 47

Chapter 5
Minimum Viable Products and Prototypes 75

Chapter 6
Feedback and Research **95**

PART III: LEAN UX IN YOUR ORGANIZATION

Chapter 7
Integrating Lean UX and Agile **117**

Chapter 8
Making Organizational Shifts **137**

Chapter 9
Case Studies **153**

Index **173**

Foreword

In reading *Lean UX*, you're about to embark on a tour of a new way of working. For those of us steeped in traditional management techniques, it may seem a little disorienting. I sometimes like to imagine what it would be like to have a bird's-eye view of the typical modern corporation. From on high, you could examine each silo of functional excellence one at a time. See them in your mind's eye: Marketing, Operations, Manufacturing, IT, Engineering, Design, and on and on in a tidy row of crisp, well-run silos.

Let's imagine you reached down to grab one of these silos and popped its top off to see inside. What would you see? This being a modern company, you'd see each silo designed for maximum efficiency. To achieve this efficiency, you'd likely find a highly iterative, customer-centric approach to problem solving. In Manufacturing, you'd encounter traditional lean thinking. In Engineering or IT, perhaps some variation on agile development. In Marketing, customer development. In Operations, DevOps. And of course in Design, the latest in design thinking, interaction design, and user research techniques.

Zooming back out to our high perch, we might be forgiven for thinking "This company uses a variety of rigorous, hypothesis-driven, customer-centric, and iterative methodologies. Surely, it must be an extremely agile company, capable of reacting quickly to changes in market conditions and continuously innovating!" But those of us who work in modern companies know how far this is from the truth.

How is it possible that our departmental silos are operating with agility, but our companies are hopelessly rigid and slow? From our far-off vantage point, we have missed something essential. Although our departments may value agility, the *interconnections* between them are still mired in an antiquated industrial past.

Consider just one example, which I hope will sound familiar. A company decides it must innovate to survive. It commissions a design team (either in-house or external) to investigate the future of its industry and recommend innovative new products that could secure its future. A period of great excitement commences. Customers are interviewed, observed, analyzed. Experiments, surveys, focus groups, prototypes, and smoke tests follow one after the other. Concepts are rapidly conceived, tested, rejected, and refined.

And what happens at the end of this process? The designers proudly present—and the business enthusiastically celebrates—a massive specification document with their findings and recommendations. The iteration, experimentation, and discovery ceases. Now Engineering is called upon to execute this plan. And although the engineering process may be agile, the specification document is rigidly fixed. What happens if the engineers discover that the specification was unworkable or even slightly flawed? What if the concepts worked great in the lab but have no commercial appeal? What if market conditions have changed since the original "learning" took place?

I once spoke to a company who had commissioned—at terrible expense—a multiyear study of their industry. The result was an impressive "view of the future" display custom-built into their corporate headquarters. Inside this room, you could see an extrapolation of what the next 10 years would look like in their industry, complete with working demos of futuristic product concepts. You can guess what happened over the succeeding 10 years: absolutely nothing. The company rotated hundreds or thousands of executives, managers, and workers through this glimpse of the future. And in fact, 10 years later, the room no longer looks futuristic. Against all odds, their forecasts turned out to be largely accurate. And yet, the company had failed to commercialize even one of the recommendations in the attendant specification document. So I asked the company what they planned to do next; they told me they were going back to the original designers and asking them to forecast the next 10 years! The company blamed their engineers and managers for their failure to commercialize, not the designers.

When I tell this story to nondesigners, they are horrified and want to convince me that it is the fancy design firm who is to blame. When I tell it to senior executives—in both large companies and startups alike—they cringe. They are constantly deluged with complaints from every single function that they are fast and cutting edge but it is the other departments that slow the company down. When the whole company fails to find new sources of growth, there is plenty of blame to go around.

But the fault is not with the designers, or the engineers, or even the executives. The problem is the systems we use to build companies. We are still building linear organizations in a world that demands constant change. We are still building silos in a world that demands thorough collaboration. And we are still investing in analysis, arguing over specifications, and efficiently producing deliverables in a world that demands continuous experimentation in order to achieve continuous innovation.

It has been just about four years since I first began writing and speaking about a new concept called Lean Startup, and barely a year since I published *The Lean Startup: How Today's Entrepreneurs Use Continuous Innovation to Achieve Radically Successful Businesses* (Crown Business). In that time, I have seen the ideas grow and spread—from industry to industry, sector to sector, and function to function. Every time we have encountered new terrain, we have relied on farsighted leaders to help translate the core principles and develop new processes to implement them.

Lean UX is an important step in that evolution. For the first time, we have a comprehensive look at how Lean Startup principles apply in a design context. Along the way, it introduces important new tools and techniques to achieve superior collaboration, faster delivery, and—most importantly—dramatically better products.

Lean Startup is a big tent. It builds on established ideas from many disciplines, from lean manufacturing to design thinking. It gives us a common vocabulary and set of concepts that can be used to accelerate results across the whole company. We can stop wasting time arguing about who is to blame and which department should rule the day.

It is my hope that all of us will remember to heed Jeff Gothelf's call to "get out of the deliverables business" and return our focus where it belongs, enlisting the whole corporation in its most urgent task: delighting customers.

It is time to break down the silos, unite the clans, and get to work.

—Eric Ries
January 30, 2013
San Francisco, CA

Authors' Note

There are many folks who have continued to be patient, supportive, and inspirational as we set out to write the second edition of this book. We wanted to take a moment to thank them.

The core of our learning and support came from our colleagues at Neo and our experiences launching, building, growing, and sunsetting a truly pioneering consulting company. These folks include Giff Constable, Ben Burton, Jono Mallanyk, Anil Podduturi, Jonathan Irwin, Tim Lombardo, Corey Innis, David Bland, Nicole Rufuku, Ian McFarland, Rabble, Paul Wilson, Mike Doel, Gina Winkler, Ken Barker, Julia Mantel, Balin Brandt, and many more. We tried to use our own ideas to build a business that tested, expanded, invalidated, and fortified many of the tactics, techniques, and points of view we've shared with you in this book. We're grateful to our colleagues and clients and humbled by all we've learned from them.

As always, we would like to thank the many folks who have contributed material to the book. As was true the first time we wrote this book, we had more case studies and contributions than we could use, so some of the wonderful material our colleagues shared didn't fit into the manuscript. This reflects more on our writing process than the quality of the contribution. With that said, thanks to Lane Goldstone, Emily Holmes, Mikael Lindh, Helene Brinkgaard, Henriette Hosbond, James Kelway, Ann Yauger, Archie Miller, Beth Sutherland, Tony Collins, Derya Eilertsen, Bill Scott, Cody Evol, Shilpa Dhar, Jeff Harrell, Dave Cronin, Dan Harrelson, Alethea Hannemann, Kristen Teti, and Matthew Hayto.

Note: From Jeff

I'd like to continue to thank my writing and business partner Josh Seiden. Despite writing three books together, building a business, working on projects, teaching together, and hanging out socially, we continue to seek out opportunities to collaborate. I learn continuously from our partnership. I also enjoy making fun of Josh's age (hint: he's really old).

Finally, no project comes without sacrifice. This edition of the book is no different. I continue to be amazed and grateful at the love, patience, and support I've had from my family over the years since the first edition came out. My wife, Carrie, has dealt with far too many hours of me locked in my office tapping at the keyboard, in hotel rooms in foreign cities, or on the airplanes taking me to those destinations. That sacrifice is not lost on me. To my daughters, Grace and Sophie, I hope I can provide some inspiration about achieving seemingly impossible tasks and having the courage to give things a shot, even if you don't think you know what you're doing. I love you all. Thank you.

Note: From Josh

In this book, Jeff and I describe a working style that is deeply collaborative. That's my preferred style of working—I always feel that I learn more and am more effective when I'm collaborating. Whatever I've been able to contribute to this book is a result of the amazing collaborations I've been lucky enough to enjoy in my career. You all know who you are. I'm very grateful to all of you.

There is one working collaboration that I do need to call out though: it's been a real pleasure to continue to collaborate with Jeff. Jeff supplies many of the things in this partnership that I can't, including optimism about deadlines, audacity in setting goals, and tirelessness in evangelizing. He's a smart, hardworking, and egoless partner. He is not, however, funny. If that's needed, I usually have to provide it.

Thanks finally, to Vicky, Naomi, and Amanda. I love you.

From Jeff and Josh

This second version of the book is our attempt to update the material to the current state of Lean UX practice and thinking. We've had four years to experiment, iterate, and optimize the ideas and techniques originally detailed in this book and we felt it was time to share that insight with you.

Lean methods are learning methods, and we expect to be learning and discovering even more as we continue our journey as practitioners and teachers of Lean UX. As you embark or continue your travel down this path, we'd love to hear about your journey—your successes, challenges, and failures—so that we can keep learning through our collaboration with you.

Please keep in touch with us and share your thoughts. You can reach us at *jeff@jeffgothelf.com* and *josh@joshuaseiden.com*. We continue to look forward to hearing from you.

Preface

The biggest lie in software is Phase Two.

If you've spent any time building digital products in the past 20 years—regardless of your role—you've felt the sting of this lie. You set aside features and ideas for the next phase of work and then they are gone—never to be heard from again. As designers, we've had hundreds, if not thousands, of wireframes and workflows end up in this same bucket.

But were these ideas abandoned because they were flawed? Did the features that shipped actually meet customer and business goals? Or did the team simply run out of time? They never got to Phase Two.

In *The Lean Startup*, Eric Ries lays out his vision for how to ensure the ideas that have the most value get the most resources. The method Ries promotes relies on experimentation, rapid iterations of ideas, and evolutionary processes. The entire concept of Phase Two becomes moot.

The junction of Lean Startup and User Experience (UX) design—and their symbiotically beneficial coexistence—is *Lean UX*.

What Is Lean UX?

The Lean principles underlying Lean Startup apply to Lean UX in three ways. First, they help us remove waste from our UX design process. We create minimally viable conversations by moving away from heavily documented handoffs. Instead, a Lean UX process creates only the design artifacts we need to move the team's learning forward. Second, Lean principles drive us to harmonize our "system" of designers, developers, product managers, quality assurance engineers, marketers, and others in a transparent, cross-functional collaboration that brings nondesigners into our design process. Last, and perhaps most important, is the mindset shift we gain from adopting a model based on experimentation. Instead of relying on a hero designer to divine the best solution from a single point of view, we use rapid experimentation and measurement to learn quickly how well (or not) our ideas meet our goals. In all of this, the designer's role begins to evolve toward design facilitation—and with that we take on a new set of responsibilities.

Besides Lean Startup, Lean UX has two other foundations: *Design Thinking* and *Agile* development philosophies. Design Thinking helps us widen the scope of our work beyond interfaces and artifacts. Design Thinking looks at systems, and helps us apply design tools to broader problems. It relies on collaboration, iteration, making, and empathy as core to problem-solving. Agile refocuses software development on shorter cycles, delivering value regularly, and continuous learning. It seeks to get ideas (oftentimes as working software) to customers quickly, sense how these ideas are received, and to adjust frequently to new learning along the way.

Lean UX uses these foundations to break the stalemate between the speed of Agile and the need for design in the product-development lifecycle. If you've struggled to figure out how UX design can work in agile environments, Lean UX is the answer.

Lean UX breaks down the barriers that have kept software designers isolated from real business needs on the one hand and actual implementation on the other. Lean UX not only brings designers to the table, it brings our partners in business and technology to the whiteboard to work with us on the best solutions in an ongoing way.

Jeff once had a large pharmaceutical client who hired the agency he worked for at the time to redesign their ecommerce platform with the goal of increasing revenues by 15 percent. Jeff was the lead interaction designer on the team. In the vacuum of their office, Jeff and his team spent months researching the current system, supply chain, competitors, target audience, and contextual use scenarios. They researched personas and assembled strategic models. Jeff designed a new information architecture for the product catalog and crafted a brand-new shopping and checkout experience.

The project took months. And when the work was complete, the team packaged it all up into a PowerPoint slide deck. This was a formidable deck—and it had to be, considering the $600,000 price tag! The team went over to the client's office and spent an entire eight-hour day going over each and every pixel and word in that deck. When it was over, the client clapped. (They really did.) Jeff and team were relieved. The client loved the work. And Jeff's team never looked at that deck again.

Six months after that meeting, nothing had changed on the client's site. The client never looked at that deck again, either.

The moral of this story: Building a pixel-perfect specification might be a route to rake in six-figure consulting fees, but it's not a way to make a meaningful difference to a real product that is crucial to real users. It's also not the reason that any designer got into the product design business. We got in to build valuable products and services, not to write specs.

Some teams we work with today create entirely new products or services. They are not working within an existing product framework or structure. In "green field" projects like these, we are simultaneously trying to discover how this new product or service will be used, how it will behave, and how we are going to build it. It's an environment of continual change, and there isn't a lot of time or patience for planning or up-front design.

Other teams work with established products that were created with traditional design and development methods. Their challenge is different. They need to build upon existing platforms while increasing revenue and brand value. These teams usually have more resources at their disposal than a ground-floor startup, but they still have to use their resources efficiently—figuring out the best way to spend those resources to build products and services their customers actually want.

As we've been practicing Lean UX, we've learned to overcome the feeling that we are showing work in an "unfinished" or "ugly" state. We now know that our first attempt will inevitably require revision. So the sooner we get our ideas out, the sooner we can figure out what those revisions should be. Waiting too long to get that feedback is wasteful. We invest too much in the initial design and are less flexible to changes because of the effort we've already put in. Accepting the iterative nature of design (and software as a medium) requires the support of a high-functioning, collaborative team. You need to know—as a team—that you're *not* going to get it right the first time and that you're all working together to iterate your way forward.

There are many elements that affect the success of digital systems. Design is certainly an important component, but product management, engineering, marketing, legal compliance, and copywriting (to name a few) all have an impact on the system. No one discipline has all the answers. This is the nature of our digital medium. Collaboration creates better work. Revision and iteration make for better products. Within the pages of this book, we've distilled the insights and tactics that have allowed us to adopt this point of view and to create real success for product and business teams—and real satisfaction for customers.

Who Is Lean UX for?

This book is, first, for interaction designers who know they can contribute more and be more effective with their teams. But, it's also for product managers who need better ways to define their products with their teams and to validate them with their customers. It's also for developers who understand that a collaborative, Agile team environment leads to better code and more meaningful work. And, finally, it's for managers—managers of UX teams, project teams, business lines, departments, and companies—who understand the difference a great UX can make.

What's in It for You?

The book is set up in three sections.

Part I provides an overview and introduction to Lean UX and its founding principles. We lay out the reasons the evolution of the UX design process is so critical and describe Lean UX. We also discuss the underlying principles that you'll need to understand to make Lean UX successful.

Part II focuses on process. Each chapter takes a step in the Lean UX cycle and details clearly how to execute each one and why each is important. We also share examples of how we and others have done these things in the past.

Part III tackles the integration of Lean UX practices into your organization. We discuss the role of Lean UX within a typical Agile development environment. We also discuss the organizational shifts that need to take place at the corporate level, the team level, and at the individual contributor level for these ideas to truly take hold.

Our hope is that this book will deliver a wake-up call to UX designers, their colleagues, and product teams in all organizations still waiting for "Phase Two." Although the book is filled with tactics and techniques to help develop your processes, we'd like you to remember that Lean UX is, at its core, a mindset.

Jeff and Josh

INTRODUCTION AND PRINCIPLES

About Part I

In this first part, we provide an introduction to Lean UX and its founding principles. We discuss why the evolution of the product design and development process is so critical, and we describe what Lean UX is. We also discuss the underlying principles you'll need to understand to make Lean UX work in your organization.

Chapter 1 provides a brief history of product design and development and why it's time for that process to evolve.

In **Chapter 2**, we present a detailed look at the key principles that drive the Lean UX process. These principles offer a framework for a leaner product design and discovery process and also provide basic management guidelines for these teams. They are critical to the success of Lean UX and, if incorporated into your organization, will have a profound impact on your culture and on the productivity and success of your teams.

Lean UX: More Important Now Than Ever Before

It's not iteration if you do it only once.
—Jeff Patton

Design Is Always Evolving

When designers first brought their craft to software in the '80s and '90s, they approached the work in the same way they approached the earlier materials they worked with. In industrial design, print design, fashion design, or any field involving physical outputs, the manufacturing step is a critical constraint. When designing for physical materials, designers need to figure out what they're making *before* they begin production, because production is expensive. It's expensive to set up a factory floor to produce hard goods or garments. It's expensive to set up a printing press for a print run.

Working in software, designers faced new challenges. They had to figure out the grammar of this new medium, and as they did, they saw new specialties like interaction design and information architecture emerge. But the *process* by which designers practiced remained largely unchanged. They still designed products in great detail in advance, because they still had to deal with a "manufacturing" process: the work had to be duplicated onto floppy disks and CDs, which were then distributed to market in exactly the same way that physical goods were distributed. The cost of getting it wrong remained high.

Today, we face a new reality. Software production has become continuous. The Internet has changed the way we distribute software. The proliferation of mobile devices, wearables, and the Internet of Things has changed the way we consume it. We are no longer limited by a physical manufacturing process, and are able to get our digital products and services into customers' hands at a pace unheard of just five years ago.

This changes everything.

Teams are now facing intense pressure from competitors who are using techniques like Agile software development, continuous integration, and continuous deployment to radically reduce their cycle times. Take Amazon as an example. *The ecommerce giant pushes new code live to their customers every 11.6 seconds.*[1] And they are using these short cycles as a competitive advantage—releasing early and often, gaining market feedback, and iterating based on what they learn to create a continuous conversation with customers. In essence, they are *discovering* their product at the same time they are *delivering* it. This has many benefits but perhaps the two most important ones are:

- The ability to learn, continuously and quickly, how well their products are meeting customer needs
- Raising customer expectations in terms of product quality and company response times to their concerns and feedback

What's more, this new way of working is not based on expensive technologies. The platforms and services that make this possible are available for free or nearly free to just about every startup team. This exposes incumbent businesses to a threat they haven't known before. Specifically, the barriers to entry—in almost every domain—have never been lower. Without the need to "manufacture" a physical product, anyone with access to the Web can design, code, and deploy services to anyone else. Faced with these new threats, traditional "get it all figured out first" approaches are simply not workable. So what should product teams do?

It's time for a change.

Lean UX is the evolution of product design and team collaboration. It takes the best parts of the designer's toolkit, combines that with Agile software development and Lean Startup thinking, and makes all of this available to the entire product team. It allows teams to exploit this new reality to maximize learning, continuously discover the best path forward, and amplify the voice of the customer.

Lean UX is deeply collaborative and cross-functional, because designers, product managers, and software engineers no longer have the luxury of working in

---

1 YouTube, "Velocity 2011: Jon Jenkins, 'Velocity Culture'", Jun 20, 2011 (https://www.youtube.com/watch?amp;v=dxk8b9rSKOo).

isolation from each other. The days of the waterfall process are over. Work is continuous. We can't afford to wait on the work of others, nor can we keep others waiting on our work. Instead, we need daily, continuous engagement with all of our colleagues if we are going to be successful. This continuous engagement allows us to strip away heavy deliverables (and the time required to create them) in favor of techniques that build *shared understanding* with our teammates. Shared understanding allows our teams to make decisions faster and empowers us to engage in more strategic conversations. Yes, we still have the tactical responsibility of tweaking aesthetic elements, page load times, form factor and screen size compatibility, workflows, and calls to action, but we have more time to focus on more valuable activities, like gathering insight that can affect strategic choices for our product.

Lean UX also lets us change the way we talk about design. Instead of talking about features and documents, we can talk about *what works*—objectively. In this new reality, we have more access to market feedback than ever before. This allows us to reframe design conversations in terms of objective business goals. We can measure what works, learn, and adjust.

Lean UX is three things. It begins as a process change for designers and product teams. But it's much more than that. It's a culture change that lets us approach our work with humility; we acknowledge that our initial solutions will probably be wrong and use many sources of insight to continuously improve our thinking. It's also a way of organizing and managing software design and development teams to be more inclusive, collaborative, and transparent. We'll dig deeply into each of these aspects of Lean UX throughout the book.

Perhaps the best way to sum up this introduction, though, is this: *Lean UX is the way we work now.*

CHAPTER 2

Principles

Go that way. Really fast. If something gets in your way, turn!
—Better Off Dead (1985)

At the heart of Lean UX, you'll find a core set of principles that govern *design process*, *team culture*, and *team organization*. Treat these principles as a framework. Start with them to get your teams pointed in the right direction. And keep them in mind as you begin to implement the Lean UX processes we describe later in this book. It's really important to mention that Lean UX is *not* a set of rules. Instead, it's an approach that you adopt. Given the variability between industries in terms of culture, regulations, and customers, this means that you will inevitably need to adjust the processes to make them work in your organization. These principles will provide guidance to help you make those adjustments.

Ultimately, if you're able to put these principles to work you'll find that you will change your team's culture. Some will have more impact than others, and some will be more difficult to push through. Regardless, each principle detailed here will help you to build a product design organization that is more collaborative, more cross-functional, and a better fit for today's agile reality.

The Foundations of Lean UX

Lean UX stands on a number of important foundations: it's a combination of a few different schools of thought. Understanding where it comes from will help you to apply the method and find resources when you get stuck.

The first foundation of Lean UX is *user experience design*. Lean UX is, at its heart, a way of practicing user experience design. Drawing on roots in the fields of human factors and ergonomics as well as the human-centered design ideas that emerged in the 1950s with the work of industrial designers like Henry Dreyfuss, today we call these methods and mindsets *user experience design* (or just *UX*), a term credited to Don Norman.[1] UX embraces a number of design fields, including interaction design, information architecture, graphic design, and many others. But the heart of UX practice is that it begins by identifying human needs—the needs of the users of the system.

In the past decade, we've seen the rise in popularity of *Design Thinking*. Design Thinking emerged in the academy in the 1970s and 1980s and was popularized by the design firm IDEO in the early 2000s. It is a way of applying human-centered design methods to a wide range of problems. Tim Brown, CEO and president of IDEO, described Design Thinking as, "innovation powered by...direct observation of what people want and need in their lives and what they like or dislike about the way particular products are made, packaged, marketed, sold, and supported."[2]

Brown continued, "[it's] a discipline that uses the designer's sensibility and methods to match people's needs with what is technologically feasible and what a viable business strategy can convert into customer value and market opportunity."

Design Thinking is important for Lean UX because it takes the explicit position that every aspect of a business (or any other system) can be approached with design methods. It gives designers permission to work beyond their typical boundaries. It also encourages nondesigners to use design methods to solve the problems they face in their roles. So, UX and its cousin Design Thinking form the critical first foundation that encourages teams to consider human needs, collaborate across roles, and approach product design from a holistic perspective.

The next foundation of Lean UX is *Agile software development*. Software developers have been using Agile methods for years to reduce their cycle times, build a cadence of continuous learning, and deliver customer value regularly. Although Agile methods can pose process challenges for designers (that we'll show you how to solve in Part II), the core values of Agile are perfectly aligned with Lean UX. Lean UX applies the four core values of Agile development to product design:

---

1 Don Norman and Jakob Nielsen, "The Definition of User Experience", Nielsen Norman Group (https://www.nngroup.com/articles/definition-user-experience).

2 Tim Brown, "Design Thinking", Harvard Business Review, June 2008 (http://hbr.org/2008/06/design-thinking/ar/1).

1. **Individuals and interactions over processes and tools.**

   Lean UX favors collaboration and conversation over deliverables and rigid process. It engages the entire team to generate ideas from diverse points of view. It encourages the free and frequent exchange of ideas to allow the team to debate, decide, and move forward quickly.

2. **Working software over comprehensive documentation.**

   Every business problem has endless solutions, and each member of a team will have an opinion on which is best. The challenge is figuring out which solution is most viable. Sometimes, it's difficult or impossible to predict in advance which solution will work. By getting our ideas into the hands of customers (often through working software) sooner, the team can quickly assess solutions for market fit and viability.

3. **Customer collaboration over contract negotiation.**

   Collaborating with your teammates and customers builds a shared understanding of the problem space and the proposed solutions. It creates consensus behind decisions. The result? Faster iterations, real involvement in product-making, and team investment in validated learning. It also lessens dependency on heavy documentation because everyone on the team has already participated in making the decisions. Collaboration creates alignment more effectively than written communication, argument, and elaborate defense.

4. **Responding to change over following a plan.**

   The assumption in Lean UX is that the initial product designs will be wrong, so the team's goal should be to find out what they got wrong as soon as possible. As soon as the team discovers what's working and what's not, they adjust their proposals and test again. This input from the market keeps teams agile, constantly nudging them in a "more right" direction.

The final foundation of Lean UX is Eric Ries's *Lean Startup* method. Lean Startup uses a feedback loop called "build-measure-learn" to minimize project risk and get teams building and learning quickly. Teams build *Minimum Viable Products* (MVPs) and ship them quickly to begin the process of learning as early as possible.

As Eric puts it, "Lean Startup initially advocates the creation of rapid prototypes designed to test market assumptions and uses customer feedback to evolve them much faster than via more traditional software engineering practices."

He continues, "Lean Startup processes reduce waste by increasing the frequency of contact with real customers, therefore testing and avoiding incorrect market assumptions as early as possible."

Lean UX is a direct application of this philosophy to the practice of product design.

Each design is a proposed business solution—a hypothesis. Your goal is to validate the proposed solution as efficiently as possible by using customer feedback. The smallest thing you can build to test each hypothesis is your MVP. The MVP doesn't need to be made of code: it can be an approximation of the end experience—it might not even be a product! You collect what you learn from your MVP and develop your ideas. Then you do it again.

So, What Is the Definition of Lean UX?

Inspired by Lean Startup and Agile development, it's the practice of bringing the true nature of a product to light faster, in a collaborative, cross-functional way.

We work to build a shared understanding of the customer, their needs, our proposed solutions, and our definition of success.

We prioritize learning over delivery to build evidence for our decisions.

Principles

In the rest of this chapter, we'll lay out the principles behind Lean UX. As you explore this approach, keep these principles in mind. Think of your experience with Lean UX as a learning journey. Use these principles to keep yourself and your team on course.

We've organized these principles into three groups: there are principles to guide *team organization*, a set of principles to guide *process*, and a set of principles to guide *culture*.

Principles to Guide Team Organization

Let's begin by taking a look at the Lean UX principles related to team organization:

- Cross-functional teams
- Small, dedicated, colocated
- Self-sufficient and empowered
- Problem-focused team

Principle: cross-functional teams

What is it? Cross-functional teams are made up of the various disciplines involved in creating your product. Software engineering, product management, interaction design, visual design, content strategy, marketing, quality assurance —these all make up a part of Lean UX teams. Lean UX demands a high level of collaboration between these disciplines. Their involvement must be continuous from day one of the project until the end of the engagement.

Why do it? Diverse teams create better solutions, because each problem is seen from many different points of view. Creating diverse teams limits the need for gated, handoff-based ("waterfall") processes. Instead, teams can share information informally, which creates collaboration earlier in the process and drives greater team efficiency.

Principle: small, dedicated, colocated

What is it? Keep your teams small—no more than 10 total core people. Dedicate them to one project and staff it all out of the same location.

Why do it? The benefit of small teams comes down to three words: communication, focus, and camaraderie. Smaller teams are easier to keep current on project status, changes, and new learning. Dedicating your team to one project keeps team members focused on the same priorities all the time and eliminates dependencies on other teams. Having the team all in one place allows relationships to grow between colleagues.

Principle: self-sufficient and empowered

What is it? Give your teams all the capabilities they need to operate without external dependencies. Ensure that they have the tools they need to create and release software. Give them permission to figure out how to solve the problems they face and to engage with users and customers through first-hand contact.

Why do it? Teams without external dependencies are free to optimize their process for maximum efficiency. They neither want for outside resources nor do they want for external expertise. Teams that can create and release software themselves can move at a rapid pace and can maximize their learning. Finally, teams cannot learn from the market if they are not allowed to engage with the market. Teams must be able to interact with customers directly in order to get the feedback they need to create effective solutions.

Principle: problem-focused teams

What is it? A problem-focused team is one that has been given a business problem to solve, as opposed to a set of features to implement. In other words, this is a team that has been organized around an outcome.

Why do it? Assigning teams problems to solve shows trust in those teams. It allows them to come up with their own solutions and drives a deeper sense of pride and ownership in the solutions the team implements.

Principles to Guide Culture

Culture and process are inextricable. Adopting Lean UX means adopting a culture of learning and curiosity. Here are the Lean UX principles that can help guide your culture toward that end state:

- Moving from doubt to certainty
- Outcomes, not output
- Removing waste
- Shared understanding
- No rock stars, gurus, or ninjas
- Permission to fail

Principle: moving from doubt to certainty

What is it? Software development is complex and unpredictable. Because of this, Lean UX begins with the idea that everything is an assumption until we prove otherwise. As we work, we gain clarity. Thus, we are always moving from a position of doubt to one of certainty.

Why do it? Every project begins with a set of assumptions. Sometimes, these assumptions are easy to spot; sometimes we don't see them until it's too late. To eliminate the risk of investing a lot of time and effort in work that's based on bad assumptions, we begin by validating our assumptions. This means that we begin with doubt and proceed to validate what we know, as systematically and rigorously as we possibly can. In the process, our learning lets us become more certain about our positions.

Principle: outcomes, not output

What is it? Features and services are *outputs*. The goals they are meant to achieve are *outcomes*. In Lean UX, teams are trying above all to create *a meaningful and measureable change in customer behavior*: an outcome. Lean UX measures progress in terms of explicitly defined outcomes.

Why do it? When we attempt to predict which features will achieve specific outcomes, we are mostly engaging in speculation. Although it's easier to manage the launch of specific feature sets, we often can't predict if a feature will be effective until it's in the market. By managing outcomes (and the progress made toward them), we gain insight into the efficacy of the features we are building. If a feature is not performing well, we can make an objective decision as to whether it should be kept, changed, or replaced.

Principle: removing waste

What is it? One of the core tenets in Lean manufacturing is the removal of anything that doesn't lead to the ultimate goal. In Lean UX, the ultimate goal is improved outcomes; hence, anything that doesn't contribute to that is considered waste and should be removed from the team's process.

Why do it? Team resources are limited. The more a team can eliminate waste, the faster they can move. Teams want to work on the right challenges. They want to be effective. Thinking in terms of value creation and waste removal can help teams keep their laser focus where it belongs.

Principle: shared understanding

What is it? Shared understanding is the collective knowledge that builds up over time as the team works together. It's a rich understanding of the space, the product, and the customers.

Why do it? Shared understanding is the currency of Lean UX. The more a team collectively understands what they're doing and why, the less they need to debate *what* happened and can quickly move to *how* to solve for the new learning. In addition, it reduces the team's dependencies on second-hand reports and detailed documents to continue its work.

Principle: no rock stars, gurus, or ninjas

What is it? Lean UX advocates a team-based mentality. Rock stars, gurus, ninjas—we use these labels to describe individual stars. Rather than focus on star performers, Lean UX seeks team cohesion and collaboration.

Why do it? Rock stars don't share—neither their ideas nor the spotlight. Team cohesion breaks down when you add individuals with large egos who are determined to stand out and be stars. When collaboration breaks down, you lose the environment you need to create the shared understanding required to move forward effectively.

Principle: permission to fail

What is it? To find the best solution to business problems, Lean UX teams need to experiment with ideas. Most of these ideas will fail. *Permission to fail* means that the team has a safe environment in which to experiment. That applies to both the technical environment (they can push out ideas in a safe way), and the cultural environment (they won't be penalized for trying ideas that don't succeed).

Why do it? Permission to fail is the platform on which you build a culture of experimentation. Experimentation breeds creativity. Creativity, in turn, yields innovative solutions. When teams don't fear for their jobs if they get something wrong, they're more apt to take risks. It is from those risks that big ideas ultimately come.

The Virtues of Continuous Improvement

In a video called "Why You Need to Fail," CD Baby founder Derek Sivers describes the surprising results of a ceramics class.[3]

On the first day, the instructor announced to his class that the students would be divided into two groups. Half of the students would only need to make one clay pot each during the semester. Their grades would depend on the perfection of that solitary pot. The other half of the class would be graded simply by the *weight* of the pots they made during the semester. If they made 50 pounds of pots or more, they'd get an A. Forty pounds would earn a B; 30 pounds, a C; and so on. What they actually made was irrelevant. The instructor said he wouldn't even look at their pots. He would simply bring his bathroom scale to the final day of class and weigh the students' work.

At the end of the semester, an interesting thing had occurred. Outside observers of the class noted that the highest-quality pots had been made by the "quantity group." They had spent the entire semester working as quickly as they could to make pots. Sometimes they succeeded, and sometimes they failed. With each iteration, each experiment, they learned. From that learning they became better able to achieve the end goal: making high-quality clay pots.

By contrast, the group that made one object didn't have the benefit of those failed iterations and didn't learn quickly enough to perform at the same level as the "quantity group." They had spent their semester theorizing about what would make a "grade-A" clay pot but didn't have the experience to execute that grandiose vision.

Principles to Guide Process

Now that we have a sense of the broader organizational and cultural principles, let's take a tactical look at how teams need to change the way they're working:

- Work in small batches to mitigate risk
- Continuous discovery
- GOOB: the new user-centricity

---

3 YouTube, "Why You Need to Fail - by Derek Sivers", Feb 15, 2011 (http://www.youtube.com/watch?v=HhxcFGuKOys).

- Externalizing your work
- Making over analysis
- Getting out of the deliverables business

Principle: work in small batches to mitigate risk

What is it? Another fundamental from Lean manufacturing is the practice of dividing work into small units, or *batches*. Lean manufacturing uses this notion to keep inventory low and quality high. Translated to Lean UX, this means creating only the design that is necessary to move the team forward and avoiding a big "inventory" of untested and unimplemented design ideas.

Why do it? Every project begins with assumptions. Large-batch design begins with those untested assumptions and creates a lot of design work on top of them. This means that if we find out that a foundational assumption is wrong, we must throw away a lot of work. By working in smaller batches, we can design and validate our decisions as we go, which reduces the risk of wasted work.

Principle: continuous discovery

What is it? Continuous discovery is the ongoing process of engaging the customer during the design and development process. This is done through regularly scheduled activities, using both quantitative and qualitative methods. The goal is to understand both *what* the user is doing with your products and *why* they are doing it. So you do research on a frequent basis and a regular rhythm. Research involves the entire team.

Why do it? Regular customer conversations provide frequent opportunities for validating new product ideas. By bringing the entire team into the research cycle, it develops empathy for users and the problems they face. You create shared understanding. Finally, as the team learns together, you reduce the need for future debrief conversations and documentation.

Principle: GOOB: the new user-centricity

What is it? It might sound like baby's first word, but GOOB is actually an acronym for what Steve Blank, Stanford professor, entrepreneur, and author, calls "getting out of the building." This is Blank's name for the kind of user and customer research that the UX community has advocated for years.

In Blank, the UX community has a champion from the business world. Blank realized that the endless meeting room debates about the customer couldn't be settled inside the office. Blank's prescription: give potential customers a chance to provide feedback on your ideas sooner than you would have in the past. Much sooner. Test your ideas with a strong dose of reality while they're still young. Better to find out that your ideas are missing the mark before you've spent time and resources building a product that no one wants.

Why do it? Ultimately, the success or failure of your product isn't the team's decision—it's the customer's. They will need to click that "Buy Now" button you designed. The sooner you give them a voice, the sooner you'll learn whether you've got an idea that works.

Principle: externalizing your work

What is it? Externalizing means getting your work out of your head and out of your computer and into public view. Teams use whiteboards, virtual shared spaces, foam-core boards, artifact walls, printouts, and sticky notes to expose their work in progress to their teammates, colleagues, and customers.

Why do it? Externalizing work allows everyone to see where the team stands. It creates a passive, ambient flow of information across the team. It inspires new ideas that build off the ones that have already been shared. It allows all the members of the team—even the quiet ones—to participate in information-sharing activities. Their sticky notes or whiteboard sketches are equally as loud as the most prominent person on the team.

Principle: making over analysis

What is it? Lean UX values making over analysis. There is more value in creating the first version of an idea than spending half a day debating its merits in a conference room.

Why do it? The answer to most difficult questions the team will face will not be answered in a conference room; it's the customers in the field who will answer them. To get those answers, you need to make the ideas concrete—you need to make something for people to respond to. Debating ideas without market-based data is waste. Instead of analyzing potential scenarios, make something and get out of the building with it.

Principle: getting out of the deliverables business

What is it? Lean UX shifts the focus of the design process away from the documents the team is creating. Instead, it focuses on the outcomes the team is achieving. With increased cross-functional collaboration, stakeholder conversation becomes less about what artifact is being created and more about which outcome is being achieved.

Why do it? Documents don't solve customer problems—good products do. The team's focus should be on learning which features have the biggest impact on its customers. The artifacts the team uses to gain and communicate that knowledge are irrelevant. All that matters is the quality of the product, as measured by the market's reaction to it.

Wrapping Up

This chapter put forward a set of foundational principles for Lean UX. These are the core attributes that any Lean UX team should strive to embody. As you begin to form your practice, we encourage you to use these principles to define your team's make up, location, goals, and practices.

In Part II, we put these principles into action as we detail the entire Lean UX process.

PART II

PROCESS

It's Tuesday, and Rick, Mark, Olga, and Arti are standing at the whiteboard, looking at a wireframe that they've drawn. Arti has a marker in her hand, but she's not drawing. "Rick, I don't understand what you're driving at. Can you explain the problem?" she asks.

Rick takes the marker, wipes clear a section of the board, and explains the regulation, again. The team is designing an app for stock traders, and the app must obey a strict set of regulations. Rick, the business analyst, is responsible for making sure that the team's designs support the rules.

After a while, the team is nodding, and Arti takes the marker again. She suggests a change to the wireframe design of the app on the board and the team nods again. They all take out their iPhones, take photos of the board, and agree to reconvene the next day. They're confident that what they've agreed on will be ready for user-testing on Thursday.

Arti, the designer, goes back to her desk to begin detailing out the design they've sketched. Mark, the frontend developer, begins building the page—he uses components from the Design System the team has built, so he doesn't need to wait for Arti before getting the basic pieces in place. Rick opens the project's wiki page and begins to document the decisions the team has made about the application's behavior. He'll review these choices with the product owner later in the day. And Olga, the QA tester, begins the process of writing tests for the new section of the app.

This is the day-to-day rhythm of Lean UX: a team working collaboratively, iteratively, and in parallel, with few handoffs, minimal deliverables, and a focus on working software and market feedback. In this section, you'll see how it's done.

About Part II

In the previous part, we looked at the ideas behind Lean UX—the principles that drive the work. In this section, we get very practical and describe in detail the process of doing Lean UX.

The Lean UX Process

Chapter 3 describes how to frame our work. Lean UX radically shifts the way we frame our work. Our goal is not to create a deliverable. It's to change something in the world—to create an outcome. In this chapter, we describe the key tools we use to do this: hypothesis statements.

Chapter 4 describes the shift in our design process. Lean UX uses many techniques familiar to designers but shifts the emphasis of our work. We become more collaborative. We aim for speed first. We prioritize learning. We use a key tool to achieve this: the Minimum Viable Product.

Chapter 5 is about experiments. Lean UX is based on the idea that we begin our work with an assumption. We use experiments to test our assumptions and then build on what we learn in those experiments. This chapter shows you how to orient your design process around experiments and learning.

Chapter 6 is about feedback. UX in any form requires good input from users. Lean UX puts a premium on continuous feedback to help guide our design process. This chapter shows you techniques that Lean UX teams use to get feedback early and often and how to incorporate that feedback into future product iterations.

CHAPTER 3

Driving Vision with Outcomes

If it disagrees with experiment, it's wrong.
—Dr. Richard Feynman

Traditionally, software projects are framed by requirements and deliverables. Teams are given requirements and are expected to produce deliverables that describe how the features that satisfy those requirements will look, behave, and perform. In many cases, the strategic context for those requirements is not communicated, is missing, or is simply not considered. Lean UX radically shifts the way we frame our work by introducing back the strategic context for our feature and design choices and, more important, how we—the entire team, not just the design department—define success. Our goal is not to create a deliverable or a feature: it's to positively affect customer behavior or change in the world—to create an outcome.

Why focus on outcomes instead of features? It's because we've learned that it's hard—and in many cases impossible—to predict whether the features we design and build will create both the strategic as well as tactical value we want to create. *Will this button encourage people to purchase? Will this feature create more engagement? Will people use this feature in ways we didn't predict? Will we successfully shift the way people interact with our service?* So, rather than focus on the feature, it's better to focus on the value we're trying to create, and keep testing solutions until we find one that delivers the value—*the outcome*—that we desire.

This reframing requires an organization-wide position of humility. It requires teams and managers to use their knowledge and skills and creativity as scientists might: they propose their best solution and then they test to see if they're right. To reduce the risk of investing too heavily in the wrong features, designs, and engineering implementations, we soften our stance from what is "required" to what is "assumed" to be true. These assumptions—still very much loaded with risk—are our best guess given our current state of knowledge. We know that as we begin to research, design, develop, and test, new information will be revealed, and this new information will undoubtedly force course corrections. It's for these reasons that we begin with outcomes and assumptions instead of features and requirements.

Using the Right Words

Language, in this case, is important. Requirements present a seemingly immutable path forward. Assumptions explicitly admit that we might be wrong. We use our assumptions to create and test hypotheses. If you're familiar with Test-Driven Development (TDD), hypotheses are very similar. They are, in a way, a form of Test-Driven Product Design and Development. We write the test first—the hypothesis. We design and/or develop just enough product (i.e., experiments and Minimum Viable Products [MVPs]) to see if the hypothesis is true. These small tests reduce the risk of going too far forward in the wrong direction. We use objective measures of customer behavior to determine if we've achieved our desired outcomes. It is these outcomes that are our definition of progress and ultimately, our new definition of done. Figure 3-1 offers an overview of the process.

This chapter digs into the main tool of outcome-focused work: the *hypothesis statement*. The hypothesis statement is the starting point for a project. It states a clear strategic vision for the work and shifts the conversation between teams, managers, and stakeholders from outputs (e.g., "We will build an iPhone app") to outcomes (e.g., "We want to increase the amount of commerce that comes through our mobile channels.")

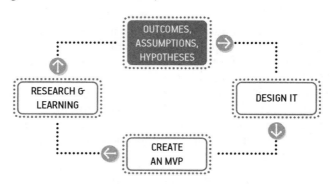

Figure 3-1. *The Lean UX process*

Assumptions

Assumptions are our best guess based on what we know today. They are also filled with risk. Your goal as Lean UX practitioners is to reduce risk.

"We believe our primary user base should be middle school and high school students who would rather use their mobile device over any other to access school content."

"We believe integrating the default calendar application on our users' mobile devices is a feature they will value and use often."

"If our users communicate with one another regularly using our app, it's an indication that we built and designed the right features."

Without the evidence to confirm these statements, they are all assumptions, filled with risk. Every downstream decision we make based on untested assumptions increases the risk of failure in our product. So when we find an assumption, we need to ask, *How might we ensure that these statements are true as quickly (and cheaply) as possible so that future decisions stand a better chance of succeeding?*

To do so, the first step in the Lean UX process is to explicitly declare your assumptions. Every project starts with assumptions, but mostly we don't acknowledge this fact. Instead, we try to ignore assumptions, or worse, treat them as facts.

Declaring your assumptions allows your team to create a common starting point. By doing this as a team, you give every team member—designer and nondesigner alike—the opportunity to ask questions about your target audience, what problems you're solving for those people, and how best to solve the problem. It allows the broader group to include concerns about things that might have been missed when the project was framed. This could include technical dependencies, competitive market concerns, or long-term service sustainability issues such as sourcing content. Most important, declaring your assumptions brings a group perspective to what success looks like.

Assumptions: The Big Four

There are four types of assumptions that are particularly important in Lean UX:

Business outcomes
> Our success metric and definition of "done." Business outcomes describe a measurable change we want to see in the world or in customer behavior. They are the signal we seek from the market to help us validate or invalidate our hypotheses. These are often quantitative but can also be qualitative.

Users
> The people for whom we believe we are solving a problem, often modeled as personas.

User outcomes
> The goals of the people for whom we are building products. These can be end goals (e.g., completing a specific task), emotional or experience goals (e.g., not feeling like a technological luddite), or long-term goals (e.g., keep as much of my money so I can retire comfortably).

Features
> These are the product changes, additions, or improvements we believe will help our customers achieve their goals and drive the business outcomes we seek.

Each of these elements is critical to writing a testable hypothesis, as we'll see later. For now, let's take a detailed look at one way to find assumptions together as a team.

Method: Declaring Assumptions

Who

Declaring assumptions is best done as a group exercise. Gather your team, making sure that all disciplines are represented—including any subject matter experts that could have vital knowledge about your project. For example, if you're handling a frequent customer complaint, it might be beneficial to include a customer service representative from your call center. Call center reps speak to more customers than anyone else in the organization and will likely have insight the rest of the team won't. By working together in this cross-functional capacity you are raising the *Product IQ* of the entire team. Team members not only get to voice their opinions and concerns, but equally as important, they get to hear other points of view. This moves team members away from discipline-specific views of the product to a more holistic, product-focused one.

Preparation

Give the team advance notice of the problem they will be taking on. Provide them the strategic context for the work to ensure that their tactics agree with the broader goals of the organization. This gives everyone a chance to prepare any material they need, ask questions, or do any research before you begin. Important things to prepare in advance include the following:

- Analytics reports that show how the current product is being used
- Usability reports that illustrate why customers are taking certain actions in your product
- Information about past attempts to fix this issue and their successes and failures
- Justification from the business as to how solving this problem will affect the company's performance
- Competitive analyses that show how your competition is tackling the same issues

Problem Statement

The team needs to have a starting point for the exercise. We've found it helpful to begin with a problem statement. (See the templates for this statement that follow.) These statements are created by key stakeholders as they begin to address the strategic vision for the business. The problem statement gives your team a clear focus for their work. It also defines any important constraints. You need constraints for group work. They provide the guardrails that keep the team grounded and aligned. Creativity thrives in the constraints.

Problem statements take on slightly different flavors depending on whether you are working on an existing product or creating a brand new one. Let's take a look at each.

Existing product: problem statement template

Problem statements for existing products are made up of three elements:

- The current goals of the product or system
- The problem the business wants addressed (i.e., where the goals aren't being met)
- An explicit request for improvement that doesn't dictate a specific solution

You can use the template shown in Figure 3-2 to express your problem statement. Keep in mind though that there's nothing magical about this template—or really any of the templates we share in this book. You should adapt the templates so that they make sense to you, your team, and your context.

> **PROBLEM STATEMENT TEMPLATE (FOR EXISTING PRODUCTS/SERVICES)**
>
> [Our service/product] is intended to achieve [these goals].
>
> We have observed that the product/service isn't meeting [these goals] which is causing [this adverse effect] to our business.
>
> How might we improve [service/product] so that our customers are more successful based on [these measurable criteria]?

Figure 3-2. *Problem statement template for existing products and services*

All too often, teams are tasked with poorly worded business problem statements. In fact, these are rarely problem statements at all. They are typically poorly hidden requirements requests. Take this "problem statement," for example:

> Our competitors have all shipped mobile applications in the past 12 months and are advertising them heavily. With the ongoing need to stay competitive, we too must develop more mobile products.
>
> To achieve this, we intend to launch an iOS application by Q2 of this year and ensure that all of our marketing sites are mobile-friendly by the beginning of Q3. In addition, we will launch a Facebook mobile ad campaign to ensure that our acquisition targets are hit this year.

This statement fails to declare a real business problem (other than feature parity concerns with our competition) nor does it indicate the impact (good or bad) this is having on the product or service. Finally, instead of providing a clear business measure of success, it lists a specific set of features and tactics the team is expected to deliver. This way of assigning work to a team does very little to raise their Product IQ or inspire any creativity in finding the right solutions. The team is tasked with a solution to implement rather than a problem to solve.

Here is an alternative version for a hypothetical company working in the educational technology space:

> Our Learning Management System (LMS) was intended to provide a central platform to facilitate communication, student body management, and assessment for parents, students, and teachers in most educational contexts.
>
> We have observed new students both in the United States and abroad entering schools with a mobile-first or mobile-only mindset. We have also

observed a significant rise in funding for competing educational technology startups catering to this new behavior model. Our products are heavy and not mobile-friendly which increases our risk of losing incoming cohorts of new students through decreased usage and dependency on the LMS.

How might we create more capable and compelling mobile offerings so that our high school and university students increase their usage of the LMS through their preferred mobile device?

This version of the problem statement sets a clear issue for the team to solve. It provides the source of the concern and a sense of the impact it might have on the company's business and ultimate success. Finally, it provides clear guidelines for how the team should proceed without dictating a specific set of features for them to build, instead opting for an outcome, a change in customer behavior, for them to achieve.

New product: problem statement template

Problem statements for new products are also made up of three elements (see Figure 3-3):

- The current state of the market
- The opportunity the business wants to exploit (i.e., where current solutions are failing)
- A strategic vision for a product or service to address the market gap

PROBLEM STATEMENT TEMPLATE (FOR NEW PRODUCTS/SERVICES)

The current state of the **[domain]** has focused primarily on **[customer segments, pain points, etc]**.

What existing products/services fail to address is **[this gap]**.

Our product/service will address this gap by **[vision/strategy]**.

Our initial focus will be **[this segment]**.

Figure 3-3. *Problem statement template for new products and services*

Let's continue our example from the educational technology space and write a new product problem statement:

The current state of the educational technology market has focused primarily on selling large installations to school systems focused on making teachers' and administrators' lives simpler. These services were created in a desktop world and serve only the providers of education, not the students. These services fail to capture the way incoming students use technology today—a mobile-first or, in some cases, mobile-only consumption pattern. Our new

Learning Management System product will address this gap by building mobile-friendly learning experiences tailored to the way primary and secondary school students use technology today as well as how they learn.

Regardless of which type of product you're working on or who created them, problem statements are also filled with assumptions. The team's job is to dissect the problem statement into its core assumptions. Here's how to do that.

Running the Exercise: Business Assumptions Exercise

We like to use this exercise (created by our friend Giff Constable) to facilitate the assumptions discussion.

Step 1: Complete the assumptions exercise individually
Each member of your team should prepare answers for the questions that follow on their own. This includes your clients.

Step 2: Share your answers
Get together with your team (and client) to kick off the new initiative. Go around the table sharing everyone's answers to the assumptions exercise, question by question.

Step 3: Collect, organize, prioritize
Collect these answers on sticky notes or a whiteboard and sort them into themes. As a team, attempt to prioritize which themes are most important for each question. Don't worry if you get to the end of the exercise without clear agreement on all of the answers. The goal is to collect statements that reflect what you and your team *think might be true*. If you have strong disagreement on a point, capture the different perspectives.

Assumptions Worksheets

BUSINESS ASSUMPTIONS

1. I believe my customers have a need to: _____

2. These needs can be solved with: _____

3. My initial customers are (or will be): _____

4. The #1 value a customer wants to get out of my service is: _____

5. They can also get these additional benefits: _____

6. I will acquire the majority of my customers through: _____

7. I will make money by: _____

8. My primary competition in the market will be: _____

9. We will beat them due to: _____

10. My biggest product risk is: _____

11. We will solve this through: _____

12. We will know we are successful when we see the following changes in customer behavior:

_____

13. What other assumptions do we have that, if proven false, will cause our business/project to fail:

_____

USER ASSUMPTIONS

1. Who is the user? _____

2. Where does our product fit in their work or life? _____

3. What problems does our product solve? _____

4. When and how is our product used? _____

5. What features are important? _____

6. How should our product look and behave? _____

You might discover that some of these questions don't apply to your project. That's OK —you can adapt the questions to your situation as you see fit. If you're early in the life of your product, you'll probably spend more time on the business assumptions. If you've got a mature product, you'll probably focus your energies on the user assumptions. The point is to cast a broad net and look for assumptions in all dimensions of your project.

When you've completed the exercise, you will have a list of assumptions. Your next step is to assemble these assumptions into hypotheses.

Hypotheses

With our assumptions in hand, we're ready to move to the next step: writing hypotheses. To do that, we transform our assumptions into a format that is easier to test: the hypothesis statement.

Generally, hypothesis statements use this format:

> *We believe* [this statement is true].
>
> *We will know we're* [right/wrong] *when we see the following feedback from the market:*
>
> [qualitative feedback] *and/or* [quantitative feedback] *and/or* [key performance indicator change].

You can see that this format has two parts. A statement of what you believe to be true, and statement of the market feedback you're looking for to confirm that you're right.

Expressing your assumptions this way turns out to be a powerful technique. It takes much of the subjective and political conversation out of the decision-making process and instead orients the team toward evidence collected from the market. In other words, it orients the team toward their users and customers.

Data-Informed Design versus Data-Driven Design

There's been a lot of backlash in the design world about data-driven design. The argument is that by reducing every design decision to factors that can be measured, it takes the delight and soul out of our products. We actually agree with this perspective, which is why we think it's so important to include qualitative targets in your success criteria. Qualitative insight helps us to understand the emotional aspects of product design. It provides the "why" to give context to the quantitative "what" insights provided by analytics tools. It gives us a sense of what's driving the behavior and provides guidance for design improvements that improve the experience. This makes our customers as well as our business more successful. By balancing qualitative and quantitative insights, we are using data to inform rather than dictate our design decisions.

Hypotheses: Tactical and Testable

At their highest levels, hypotheses can seem daunting. Where do you begin? What do you test first? In these situations, we've found it helpful to focus our hypothesis writing on features. Figure 3-4 presents the format we recommend for articulating tactical, testable hypothesis statements.

FEATURE HYPOTHESIS STATEMENT TEMPLATE

We believe this **[business outcome]** will be achieved
if **[these users]** successfully achieve **[this user outcome]**
with **[this feature]**.

Figure 3-4. *Feature hypothesis template*

The first field is completed with the outcome you've determined is your measure of success. This is the business outcome you'd like to achieve. The second field describes exactly which of your target users you believe you should focus on first. The third field speaks to the end goal, benefit, or the emotional state those customers will get if we design and implement our feature well. The final field speaks to the way we believe we should improve our product or the new features we'd like to build.

It's easy to jump to features first. Most teams do this. By structuring your conversations with hypotheses you force the team to think through the context first, and especially, the problem you're trying to solve. This constrains the space for determining which features to work on. Each assumption you put in place increasingly confines the team's thinking to a more accurate set of potential features. This focus makes any feature discussion more productive, more targeted, and ultimately more relevant to your customers.

Getting from Problem Statement to Hypothesis

Let's take a look at an example of how this works by going back to the problem statement we looked at earlier:

> Our Learning Management System (LMS) was intended to provide a central platform to facilitate communication, student body management, and assessment for parents, students, and teachers in most educational contexts. We have observed new students both in the United States and abroad entering schools with a mobile-first or mobile-only mindset. We have also observed a significant rise in funding for competing educational technology startups catering to this new behavior model. Our products are heavy and not mobile-friendly which increases our risk of losing incoming cohorts of new students through decreased usage and dependency on the LMS.
>
> How might we create more capable and compelling mobile offerings so that our high school and university students increase their usage of the LMS through their preferred mobile device?

The team working on this problem knows that if they don't meet the needs of an increasingly mobile user base, they will lose business. They need to figure out how to increase mobile use of the system by students. The team's first step is to declare their assumptions and then write a set of testable hypotheses for this problem.

Completing Your Hypothesis Statements

To create your hypothesis statements, you will need to begin assembling the building blocks. Here is what you are going to want to put together:

- The *business outcomes* you are trying to achieve
- The *users* you are trying to service
- The *user outcomes* that motivate them
- The *features* you believe might work in this situation

After you have all of this raw material, you can put them all together into a set of statements. Let's take a closer look at each of these elements.

Running the exercise: business outcomes

Business outcomes are your definition of done. They are the result your business seeks, and the measuring stick for success. When you manage with outcomes, the question isn't, "Did you ship it?" Instead, the question is, "How did this create a good result for us, for the customer, or for us both?" When you're creating hypotheses to test, you want to try to be very specific regarding the outcomes you are trying to create. We discussed earlier how Lean UX teams focus less on output (the documents, sketches, products, and features that we create) and more on the outcomes that these outputs create. *Can we make it easier for people to log in to our site? Can we encourage more people to sign up? Can we encourage greater collaboration among system users?*

Together with your team, look at the problem you are trying to solve. You probably have a few high-level outcomes that you are trying to create (increasing sign-ups, increasing usage, etc.). Consider how you can break down these high-level outcomes into smaller parts. What behaviors will predict greater usage? More visitors to the site? More downloads of your app? Increasing number of items in the shopping cart? Sometimes, it's helpful to run a team brainstorm to create a list of possible outcomes that you believe will predict the larger outcome you seek.

In the example in Figure 3-5 (from Giff Constable), an executive leadership team brainstormed and then voted on which Key Performance Indicators (KPIs) the company should pursue next. After consolidating down to the list shown in the photo, each executive was given four M&M's. As long as they managed not to eat their votes, these executives were able to vote with candy for each metric they felt was most important. Ties were broken by the CEO.

Figure 3-5. *Brainstorming a list of possible outcomes*

Another way to get to your initial business outcomes is to use a framework called "Startup Metrics for Pirates." Created by Dave McClure, an early employee of PayPal and the founder of 500 Startups, this framework is based on a customer lifecycle funnel (Figure 3-6). New customers come into the top of the funnel and move through increasing stages of engagement with a business. It also talks about pirates, which is fun.

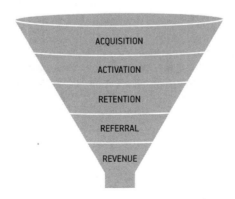

Figure 3-6. *Dave McClure's Startup Metrics for Pirates*

The Startup Metrics for Pirates framework is condensed into the acronym AARRR (Pirates!) and, when expanded, looks like this:

Acquisition
Can we get customers to our new feature or product?

Activation
After we get them there, can we get them to use it?

Retention
Can we get them to use it again? And again?

Referral
Can we get them to tell their friends, colleagues, bosses, or others about it?

Revenue
Can we get them to pay us for this feature?

Each step in this framework indicates a greater level of engagement from your customers. And, in a digital product or service, these are all measurable behaviors, which means they serve as great business outcomes to determine the initial traction of your efforts and where to focus your optimization efforts.

Output, Outcome, and Impact

We've talked a lot in this chapter about outcomes as the measure of success for your product. One challenge we've observed with the teams we've worked with is finding the right level of granularity in determining the right outcomes to measure. To help with that, let's look at three different measures of success:

Output
These are features we design, implement, and ship. As a measure of success they are very common because they are clearly visible and easy to measure (you either shipped the feature or you didn't). What they don't measure is value to the customer. They only capture the team's delivery performance.

Outcome
This is the change in the world we hope to see after we've created the output. As a measure of success, these are rare primarily because they are not binary and instead operate on a sliding scale. If a team is asked to improve retention by 50% but only manages to improve it by 42%, does that mean they've failed? It's not always clear.

Impact
These are high-level measures of business health. Most companies measure these in the form of revenue, profits, sales, Net Promoter Score, and so on. As a measure of team-level success, these are usually too high level because it is often difficult to attribute a direct correlation between the launch of a tactical feature or a sys-

---

tem optimization and an impact-level improvement. There are far too many factors that regularly affect these measures.

It is therefore in your best interest to ask your teams to work on outcome-level metrics. It's at this level of granularity that teams can draw direct correlation between work they are doing and explicit changes in customer behavior.

Running the exercise: users

If your team already has a well-defined set of personas, the only thing you need to consider at this point is which ones you will be using in your hypothesis statements. If it's been a while since you last reviewed your personas, things might have changed. This makes for a great opportunity to ensure that they are still relevant and that you and your colleagues still believe they are representative of your target audience. If you don't have personas yet, though, this section will tell you how we like to create personas for the Lean UX process.

Proto-Personas

Designers have long been advocates for the end user. Lean UX doesn't change that. As we make assumptions about our business and the outcomes we'd like to achieve, we still need to keep the user front and center in our thinking.

Most of us learned to think about personas as a tool to represent what we learned in our research. And it was often the case that we created personas as the output of lengthy, expensive research studies. There are a few problems with personas that are created this way. First, we tend to regard them as untouchable because of all of the work that went into creating them. In addition, it's often the case that these personas were created by a research team or third-party vendor. This creates a risky knowledge gap between the people who conducted the research and those who are using the personas.

In Lean UX, we change the order of operations in the persona process. We also change persona-creation from a one-time activity to an ongoing process—one that takes place whenever we learn something new about our users.

When creating personas in this approach, we *start* with assumptions and *then* do research to validate our assumption. Instead of spending months in the field interviewing people, we spend a few hours creating proto-personas. Proto-personas are our best guess as to who is using (or will use) our product and why. We sketch them on paper (Figure 3-7) with the entire team contributing—we want to capture everyone's assumptions. Then, as we conduct ongoing research, we quickly find out how accurate our initial guesses are and we adjust our personas in response.

Figure 3-7. *A proto-persona sketch*

Besides putting the customer front and center for a diverse product development team, proto-personas serve two more key purposes:

Shared understanding
Imagine your team sitting around a table and someone says the word "dog." What image comes to your mind? Is it the same image that comes to your colleagues' minds (Figure 3-8)? How do you know?
The same thing happens when someone says "the customer." The proto-persona approach ensures that everyone has the same image in their head when "the user" is invoked.

Figure 3-8. *Dogs. (We are indebted to our esteemed colleague Adrian Howard for this concept.)*

Remembering we are not the user

It is often easy to assume our users are like us—especially if we consume the products we make. The reality is that we have a level of understanding and tolerance for the digital ecosystem that our customers rarely share. Going through a proto-persona exercise puts the focus on external users, pushing the team further away from their personal preferences for the product.

Using Proto-Personas

A team we were working with in New York was building an app that improved the Community Supported Agriculture (CSA) experience for New York City residents. CSA is a program that allows city residents to pool their money and purchase an entire season's worth of produce from a local farmer. The farmer then delivers his crops, weekly, to the members of the CSA. Many subscribers to the CSA are men and women in their late 20s and early 30s who need to juggle a busy work life, an active social life, and a desire to participate in the CSA.

The team assumed that most CSA consumers were women who liked to cook. They spent about an hour creating a persona named Susan. But when they went out into the field to do research, they quickly learned that the overwhelming majority of cooks, and hence potential users of their app, were young men. They returned to the office and revised their persona to create Anthony.

Anthony proved to be a far more accurate target user. The team had not wasted any more time refining ideas for the wrong audience. They were now focused on an audience that, while still not perfect, was far more correct than their initial assumptions.

Persona Format

We like to sketch proto-personas on paper using three hand-drawn sections (Figure 3-9). The upper-left quadrant holds a rough sketch of the persona along with her (or his) name and role. The upper-right box holds basic demographic and behavioral information. Try to focus on information that predicts a specific type of behavior—behavior relevant to our product or service. For example, there might be cases for which the persona's age is totally irrelevant, whereas her access to a specific device, like an iPhone, will completely change the way she interacts with your product.

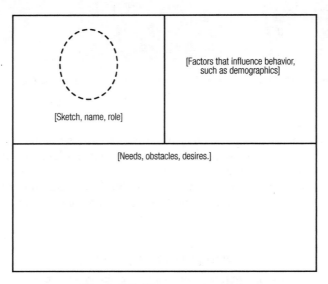

Figure 3-9. *The persona template*

The bottom half of the proto-persona is where we put the meat of the information. Here we capture the high-level needs of the persona along with the obstacles that keep her from achieving these needs. Remember that users rarely need "features." What they need is to attain some kind of goal. (It's not always a concrete goal: sometimes it's an emotional goal, an unarticulated desire, etc.) It is our job to decide how best to get them to their goals.

The Persona Creation Process

As with the other elements of the hypothesis statement, we like to start the persona creation process with a brainstorm. Team members offer up their opinions on who the project should be targeting and how that would affect their use of the product. When the brainstorming is complete, the team should narrow down the ideas to an initial set of three to four personas they believe are most likely to be their target audience. You should try to differentiate the personas around needs and roles rather than by demographic information.

After you've narrowed down the list of potential users, have the team complete the template for each one. Review this internally and, upon agreement, share with your colleagues beyond the team for their initial input. At this point in the process, you can begin to validate some of your early assumptions. Use your personas as recruiting targets to begin your research. Immediately, there are three things you can determine based on your proto-personas:

Does the customer exist?

By recruiting for the personas you created you can quickly determine how realistic your team's assumptions are. If you can't find the people you sketched, they probably don't exist. Learn from that and edit your personas.

Do they have the needs and obstacles you think they do?

In other words, are we solving real problems? You can gauge this simply by observing and speaking with the individuals you recruit. If they don't, you're building solutions for problems that don't exist—and that rarely ends well.

Would they value a solution to this problem?

Just because a customer is real and has the pain points you're solving for, this doesn't actually mean they'll value a new way to solve that problem. In other words, just because they eat bananas on their cereal every day and they don't like slicing bananas, it doesn't mean that they'll buy your banana slicer (Figure 3-10). It's important to understand how your customers are currently solving these needs and how likely your idea is to displace the incumbent solution. If you're trying to displace long-held tools like email or spreadsheets, you might be in for a tough fight. It's good to get that information sooner rather than later.

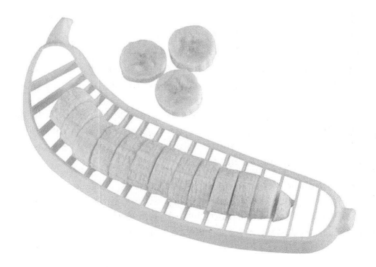

Figure 3-10. *The banana slicer*

Many teams we've worked with and heard from over the years run this proto-persona exercise; however, far fewer of them actually go back and adjust their thinking after the initial creation exercise. *It is important that you consider proto-personas to be living documents.* Each time you conduct customer conversations or usability studies, ask yourself how many of the team's current beliefs about their target audience are still true. As new information is revealed, bring it up for discussion and adjust the personas so that future research efforts can be more targeted and more successful.

Running the exercise: user outcomes

Despite the proliferation of Agile techniques like user stories, the user and their goals often become lost in the lengthy debates over features, designs, and implementations. Empathy is at the heart of great products and services. Designers often have been responsible for advocating for the user from an empathetic point of view. As we now know, this is not uniquely a designer's responsibility. To achieve broader shared understanding of users and a deeper sense of empathy for what they are trying to achieve, we ask our teams to declare their assumptions about what users are trying to do, in the form of *user outcomes*.

To do that, ask your teams the following:

- What is the user trying to accomplish? *Example: I want to buy a new phone.*

- How does the user want to feel during and after this process? *Example: I want to feel like I got the phone I need at a good price and that I'm keeping up technologically with my peers (i.e., I want to feel cool).*

- How does our product or service get the user closer to a life goal or dream? *Example: I want to feel tech-savvy and respected for it.*

Note that not every user outcome exists at all three levels. But thinking about outcomes in these terms can help you to find important dimensions of your solution to work on, from the functional, task-oriented outcomes to the more emotional experience-oriented outcomes.

User outcome brainstorming process: Again, sticky notes and whiteboards are our preferred tools here (see Figure 3-11). Allow individuals on the team to generate many ideas in silence and then organize those ideas with an affinity mapping exercise to drive the team toward convergence.

Figure 3-11. *A team brainstorming together*

Running the exercise: features

After you have a list of business outcomes in mind and have set your focus on a group of users and their needs, it's time to begin thinking about what tactics, features, products, and services you can put in place to achieve them. This is typically the part where everyone on the team has a strong opinion—after all, features are the most concrete things we work with, so it's often easiest for us to express our ideas in terms of features. Too often, though, our design process begins when someone has a feature idea, and we forget to investigate whether the feature will create meaningful results for the business, or for its customers and users. In Lean UX, features exist to serve the needs of the customer and the business.

Feature brainstorming process: Employing the same techniques described earlier, we like to create feature lists by brainstorming them as a team. We're looking for features we think will help users achieve the *user outcomes* they seek. If the feature is just a cool idea, but not in service of a user outcome, it's unlikely to create value. For example, if you're trying to drive greater collaboration between users of your product and the team comes up with the idea of using a scan to match people with similar eye color into collaboration groups, that is unlikely to achieve the desired outcome and instead is simply an excuse for the team to solve for new technologies.

Have each team member write each idea, using a thick felt pen, on a sticky note. When time is up, ask everyone to post their notes to the wall. Finally, have the group arrange them into themes.

Running the exercise: assembling your feature hypotheses

With all of your raw material created, you're ready to organize this material into a set of tactical, testable hypotheses. We like to create a table like the one in Figure 3-12 and then complete it by using the material we've brainstormed. If you've been creating all of this raw material in a workshop context, you'll need a lot of material on sticky notes. Physically move your notes into the appropriate boxes to make rows of related ideas.

WE BELIEVE THAT:			
We will achieve	...if this user...	...can achieve...	...with this feature
[business outcome]	[persona]	[user outcome]	[feature]

Figure 3-12. *A hypothesis table*

You'll find during this exercise that there are gaps in your initial brainstorms. Some business outcomes might have no features created for them, whereas some features might not drive any value for the customer or the business. That's the point of this exercise: to make sense of your initial round of thinking. After you've identified the gaps in your brainstorms, fill them in with new sticky notes or leave the less relevant ideas off the chart, as depicted in Figure 3-13. This will help make sense of the undoubtedly large number of ideas your team generates.

Figure 3-13. *Working on the hypothesis chart*

After you've completed the chart—7 to 10 rows are a good initial target—begin extracting feature hypotheses from it. Use the hypothesis template shown in Figure 3-4 to ensure you're including all the relevant components of the hypothesis statement.

As you write your hypotheses, consider which persona(s) you're serving with your proposed solutions. It's not unusual to find solutions that serve more than one at a time. It's also not unusual to create a hypothesis in which multiple features drive similar outcomes. When you see that happening, refine the hypothesis to focus on just one feature. Hypotheses with multiple features are not easy to test. The important thing to remember in this entire process is to keep your ideas specific enough so that you can create meaningful tests to see if your ideas hold water.

Prioritizing Hypotheses

Lean UX is an exercise in ruthless prioritization. It's rare to have a project budget focused strictly on learning. In most cases, we need to ship product at some point, as well. The reason we declare our assumptions at the outset of our work is so that we can identify project risks. After we string them together into hypotheses we create a backlog of potential work. Next, we need to figure out which ones are the riskiest ones—so that we can work on them first. Understanding that you can't test every assumption, how do you decide which one to test first? We like to create a chart like the one presented in Figure 3-14 and use it to map out the list of hypotheses. The goal is to prioritize which

---

1 Mountain Goat Software, "User Stories" (https://www.mountaingoatsoftware.com/agile/user-stories).

hypotheses to test based on their level of risk (*How bad would it be if we were wrong about this?*) along with how much value we believe this idea will generate. The higher the risk and the more perceived value involved, the higher the priority is to test those hypotheses first.

This does not mean that assumptions that don't make the first cut are gone forever. Keep a backlog of the other hypotheses you've created so that you can come back to them and test them if and when it makes sense to do so.

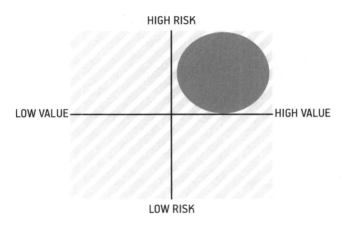

Figure 3-14. *Risk Prioritization Matrix*

Moving on to Design

When your list of hypotheses is complete and prioritized, you're ready (finally!) to move on to the next step: collaborative design. If you've gone through this process to this point with your entire team (and we strongly recommend that you do), you'll be in a great position to move forward together. This process is an effective way to create a shared understanding and shared mission across your entire team.

Wrapping Up

In this chapter we discussed how we can reframe our work in terms of outcomes. This is a vitally important Lean UX technique: framing our work with outcomes frees us (and our teams) to search for the best solutions to the problem at hand. We looked at the process of declaring assumptions and writing hypotheses. We begin with the project's problem statements and then acknowledge our assumptions. We transform these assumptions into hypotheses. We learned how to write hypothesis statements that capture our intended features, audience, and goals and that are specific enough to be tested. We end up with statements that will serve as our roadmap for the next step of the Lean UX process: collaborative design.

In the next chapter, we cover what collaborative design is and how it differs from traditional product design. We discuss specific tools and techniques that empower teams to design together and we show you how designing together is the beginning of the hypothesis testing process.

CHAPTER 4

Collaborative Design

> *As you navigate through the rest of your life, be open to collaboration. Other people and other people's ideas are often better than your own. Find a group of people who challenge and inspire you, spend a lot of time with them, and it will change your life.*
>
> **—Amy Poehler**

What is a "user experience"? It's the sum total of all of the interactions a user has with your product and service. It's created by all of the decisions that you and your team make about your product or service: the way you price it, the way you package and sell it, the way you onboard users, the way you support it and maintain it and upgrade it, and so on and so on. In other words, it's created by a team, not an individual user interface designer. For this reason, Lean UX begins with the idea that user experience design should be a collaborative process.

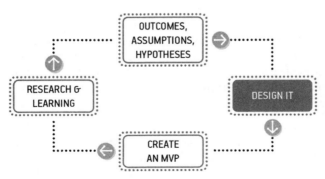

Figure 4-1. *The Lean UX cycle*

Lean UX brings designers and nondesigners together in co-creation. It yields ideas that are bigger and better than their individual contributors. But it's not design-by-committee. It's a process that is orchestrated and facilitated by designers, but one that's executed by specialists working in their individual discipline who work from a common playbook you create together. Lean UX increases your team's ownership over the work by providing an opportunity for individual points of view to be shared much earlier in the process.

In this chapter we'll explore the many benefits that come from this close, cross-functional collaboration. Specifically, we'll look at the following:

- Why everybody gets to design
- How low-fidelity artifacts increase collaboration
- Building a shared understanding across your team

We'll also look at a set of techniques that enable this more productive way of working:

- Design Studio—a collaborative sketching exercise for the entire team
- Design systems and style guides—living repositories of all the customer-facing elements of your product
- Collaboration techniques for geographically distributed teams

Let's dig in...

Collaborative Design

In Chapter 3, you learned about hypotheses. To test your hypotheses, you sometimes simply conduct research (described in Chapter 6). But other times, you need to design and build something that will help you to test these hypotheses. For example, if you're in the early stage of a project, you might test demand by creating a landing page that will measure how many customers sign up for your service. Or if you're later in the product lifecycle, you might be working at the feature level—adding some new functionality that will make users more productive, for example. Navigating the many possible design options for these features can be difficult for teams. How often have you experienced team conflict over design choices?

The most effective way we've found to rally a team around a design direction is through collaboration. Over the long haul, collaboration yields better results than hero-based design (the practice of calling in a designer or design team to drop in, come up with something beautiful, and take off to rescue the next project). Teams rarely learn or get better from working with heroes. Instead, in the same way that creating hypotheses together increases the *Product IQ* of the team, designing together increases the *Design IQ* of the team. It allows all of the members of the team to articulate their ideas. It gives designers a much broader set of ideas to draw upon as they refine the design. This, in turn, increases the entire team's feelings of ownership in the work. Finally, collaborative design builds team-wide shared understanding. It is this shared understanding that is the currency of Lean UX. The more the team collectively understands, the less it has to document in order to move forward.

Collaborative design is an approach that allows a team to design together. It helps teams build a shared understanding of both the design problem and the solution. It provides the means for them to work together to decide which functionality and interface elements best implement the feature they want to create.

Collaborative design is still a designer-led activity. It's the designer's responsibility to not only call collaborative design meetings but to facilitate them, as well. Sometimes, you'll have informal chats and sketching sessions. Sometimes, more structured one-on-one sessions with a developer at a whiteboard. Other times, you will gather the entire team for a Design Studio exercise. The key is to collaborate with a diverse group of team members.

In a typical collaborative design session, teams sketch together, critique the work as it emerges, and ultimately converge on a solution they feel has the greatest chance of success. The designer, while still producing designs, takes on the additional role of facilitator to lead the team through a series of exercises.

The output of these sessions typically consists of low-fidelity sketches and wireframes. This level of fidelity is important. First, it makes it possible for everyone to contribute, even team members with less sophisticated drawing skills. Second, it's critical to maintaining the malleability of the work. This gives the team the ability to pivot quickly if their tests reveal that the approach isn't working. It's much easier to pivot from a failed approach if you haven't spent too much time laboriously drawing, documenting, and detailing that approach.

Collaborative Design: The Informal Approach

A few years ago, Jeff was designing a dashboard for a web app targeted at TheLadders' recruiter and employer audience. There was a lot of information to fit on one screen and he was struggling to make it all work. Instead of burning too much time at his desk pushing pixels, he grabbed a whiteboard and asked Greg, the lead developer, to join him. Jeff sketched his original idea about how to lay out all of the content and functionality for this dashboard (see Figure 4-2). The two of them then discussed the idea, and eventually Jeff handed Greg the marker. He sketched his ideas on the same whiteboard. They went back and forth, ultimately converging on a layout and flow that they felt was both usable *and* feasible, given that they needed to deliver a solution within the current two-week sprint. At the end of that two-hour session, they returned to their desks and began working. Jeff refined the sketch into a more formal wireframe and workflow while Greg began to write the infrastructure code necessary to get the data they needed to the presentation layer.

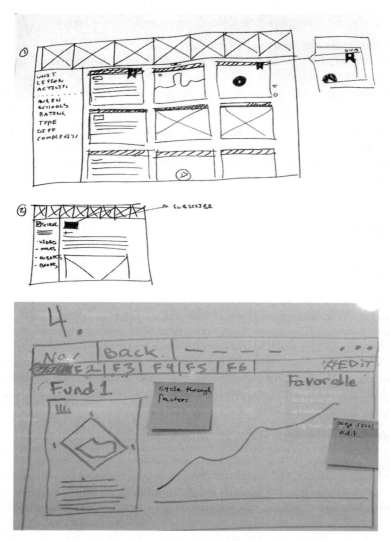

Figure 4-2. *Examples of whiteboard sketches*

They had built a shared understanding through their collaborative design session. They both knew what they were going to build and what the feature needed to do. They didn't need to wait to document it. This allowed them to get the first version of this idea built within a two-week time frame.

Conversation: Your Most Powerful Tool

Lean UX promotes conversation as the primary means of communication among team members. In this way, it is very much in line with the Agile Manifesto that promotes "Individuals and interactions over processes and tools." Conversation unites a team around a shared vision. It also brings insights from different disciplines to the project much earlier than a traditional design cycle would allow. As new ideas are formed or changes are made to the design, a team member's insight can quickly challenge those changes in a way the designer alone wouldn't have recognized.

By having these conversations early and often, the team is aware of everyone's ideas and can get started on their own work earlier. If they know that the proposed solution requires a certain backend infrastructure, for example, the team's engineers can get started on that work while the design is refined and finalized. Parallel paths for software development and design are the fastest route to reach an actual experience.

These conversations might seem awkward at first; after all, you're breaking down time-tested walls between disciplines. As the conversation evolves, however, designers provide developers with input on the implementation of certain features, ensuring the proper evolution of their vision. These conversations promote transparency of process and progress. This transparency builds a common language and deeper bonds between team members. Teammates who trust one another are more motivated to work together to produce higher-quality work.

Find ways to have more conversations with your teammates, both work-related and not. Time spent cultivating social ties with your team—eating meals together, for example—can make work-related conversations easier, more honest, and more productive.

Collaborative Design: A More Structured Approach

When your team is comfortable collaborating, informal sessions like the one we've just described take place all the time. But sometimes, you are going to need to gather everyone for a formal working session. Design Studio is a popular way to do this.[1]

---

1 In the years since we published the first edition of this book, the Design Studio method has become increasingly popular. There are now two comprehensive guides to the method. If you want to go deeper than our coverage, see *Design Sprint* by Banfield, Lombardo, and Wax (http://shop.oreilly.com/product/0636920038573.do) and *Sprint* by Knapp, Zeratsky, and Kowitz.

This method, born in the architecture world where it was called *Design Charrette*, is a way to bring a cross-functional team together to visualize potential solutions to a design problem. It breaks down organizational silos and creates a forum for your fellow teammates' points of view. By putting designers, developers, subject matter experts, product managers, business analysts, and other competencies together in the same space focused on the same challenge, you create an outcome far greater than working in silos allows. It has another benefit. It begins to build the trust your team will need to move from these formal sessions to more frequent and informal collaborations.

Running a Design Studio

The technique described in the sections that follow is very specific; however, you should feel comfortable to run less or more formal Design Studios as your situation and timing warrants. The specifics of the ritual are not the point as much as the activity of solving problems with your colleagues and clients.

Setting

To run a Design Studio session, you'll want to find a dedicated block of time within which you can bring the team together. You should plan on at least a three-hour block. You'll want a room with tables that folks can gather around. The room should have good wall space, so you can post the work in progress to the walls as you go.

The team

The process works best for a team of five to eight people. If you have more people, you can just create more teams and have the teams compare output at the end of the process. (Larger groups take a long time to get through the critique and feedback steps, so it's important to split groups larger than about eight people into smaller teams who can each go through the following process in parallel, converging at the end.)

Process

Design Studio works within the following flow:

1. Problem definition and constraints
2. Individual idea generation (diverge)
3. Presentation and critique
4. Iterate and refine in pairs (emerge)
5. Team idea generation (converge)

Supplies

Here's what you'll need:

- Pencils
- Pens
- Felt-tip markers or similar (multiple colors/thickness)
- Highlighters (multiple colors)
- Sketching templates (you can use preprinted one-up and six-up templates or you can use blank sheets of 11″ x 17″ [A3] paper divided into 6 boxes)
- 25″ x 30.5″ (A1) self-stick easel pads
- Drafting dots (or any kind of small stickers)

Problem definition and constraints (15–45 minutes)

The first step in Design Studio is to ensure that everyone is aware of the problem you are trying to solve, the assumptions you've declared, the users you are serving, the hypotheses you've generated, and the constraints within which you are working. This can be a formal presentation with slides or it can be a group discussion.

Individual idea generation (10 minutes)

You'll be working individually in this step. Give each member of the team a six-up template, which is a sheet of paper with six empty boxes on it, as depicted in Figure 4-3. You can make one by folding a blank sheet of 11″ x 17″ paper or make a preprinted template to hand to participants. (Some teams like to hand out small individual whiteboards to each participant. These are great because they're easy to erase and tend to make people feel relaxed.)

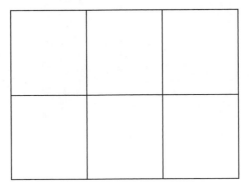

Figure 4-3. *A blank "six-up" template*

Sometimes, people find they have hard time facing a blank page. If that's the case, try this optional step. Ask everyone to label each box on their sheets with one of your personas and the specific pain point or problem they will be addressing for that persona. Write the persona's name and pain point at the top of each of the six boxes. You can write the same persona/pain point pair as many times as you have solutions for that problem or you can write a different persona/pain point combination for each box. Any combination works. Spend five minutes doing this.

Next, with your six-up sheets in front of you, give everyone five minutes to generate six, low-fidelity sketches of solutions (see Figure 4-4 and Figure 4-7) for each persona/problem pair on their six-up sheet. These should be visual articulations (UI sketches, workflows, diagrams, etc.) and not written words. Encourage your team by revealing the dirty secret of interaction design to level the playing field: If you can draw a circle, square, and a triangle, you can draw every interface. We're confident everyone on your team can draw those shapes.

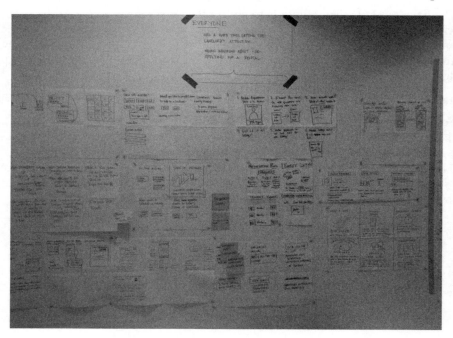

Figure 4-4. *A wall full of completed six-up drawings*

Presentation and critique (3 minutes per person)

When time is up, share and critique what you've done so far. Going around the table, give the participants three minutes to hold up their sketches and present them to the team (Figure 4-5). Presenters should explicitly state who they were solving a problem for (in other words, what persona) and which pain point they were addressing, and then explain the sketch. Each member of the team should provide critique and feedback to the presenter. Team members should focus their feedback on clarifying the presenter's intentions.

Giving good feedback is an art: In general, it's better to ask questions than to share opinions. Questions help the team talk about what they're doing, and help individuals think through their work. Opinions, on the other hand, can stop the conversation, inhibit collaboration, and put people on the defensive. So, when you're providing critique, try to use questions like, "How does this feature address the persona's specific problem?" Or, "I don't understand *that part* of the drawing. Can you elaborate?" Questions like these are very helpful. Comments such as, "I don't like that concept," provide little value and don't give the presenter concrete ideas to use for iterating.

Figure 4-5. *A team presenting and critiquing drawings during a Design Studio*

Make sure that every team member presents and receives critique.

Pair up to iterate and refine (10 minutes)

Now ask everyone to pair up for the next round. (If two people at the table had similar ideas, it's a good idea to ask them to work together.) Each pair will be working to revise their design ideas (Figure 4-6). The goal here is to pick the ideas that have the most merit and develop a more evolved, more integrated version of those ideas. Each pair will have to make some decisions about what to keep, what to change, and what to throw away. Resist the temptation here to create quick agreement by getting more general or abstract. In this step, you need to make some decisions and get *more* specific. Have each pair produce a single drawing on an 11″ x 17″ (A3) six-up sheet. Give each team 10 minutes for this step.

When the time is up, ask the team to go through the present-and-critique process again.

Figure 4-6. *A team working together in a Design Studio exercise*

Team idea generation (45 minutes)

Now that all team members have feedback on their individual ideas and people have paired up to develop ideas further, the team must converge on one idea. In this step, the team is trying to select the ideas they feel have the best chance for success. This set of ideas will serve as the basis for the next step in the Lean UX process: creating an MVP and running experiments (both covered in the next chapter).

Ask the team to use a large sheet of self-stick easel pad paper or a whiteboard to sketch the components and workflow for their idea. There will be a lot of compromise and wrangling at this stage, and to get to consensus, the team will need to prioritize and pare back features. Encourage the team to create a "parking lot" for good ideas that don't make the cut. This will make it easier to let go of ideas. Again, it's important to make decisions here: resist the temptation to get consensus by generalizing or deferring decisions.

(If you have split a large group into multiple teams in the Design Studio, ask each team to present their final idea to the room when they are finished for one final round of critique and feedback, and if desired, convergence.)

Using the output

Before you break, decide on next steps. You can use the designs you've created in this process as the basis for building MVPs, for running experiments, for production design and development—the process is very versatile. Just ensure that, having asked people to spend a lot of time contributing to the final design, you treat their contribution with respect. Decide together on next steps and then stay on top of the progress so that people keep their commitments and follow through.

To keep the output visible, post it on a design wall or another prominent place so that the team can refer back to it. Decide on what (if any) intermediate drawings people want to keep and display these alongside the final drawing, again so that team members can refer back to the ideas. Regardless of what you keep posted on the wall, it's generally a good idea to photograph *everything* and keep it in an archive folder of some sort. You never know when you'll want to go back to find something. It's also a good idea to put a single person in charge of creating this archive. Creating some accountability will tend to ensure that the team keeps good records.

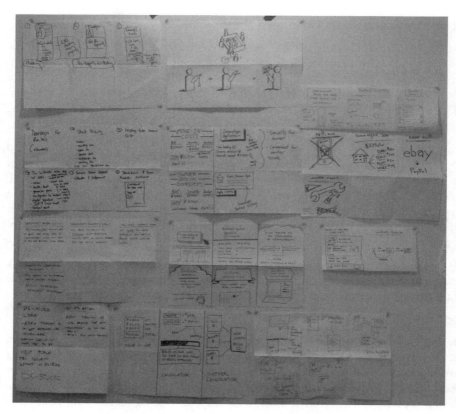

Figure 4-7. *Output of a Design Studio session*

Design Systems

So far in this chapter, we've focused on the ways that teams can design together. In practice, this usually means that teams are sketching together, either on paper or at a whiteboard. It almost never means that teams are sitting together at a workstation moving pixels around. In fact, this kind of group hovering at the pixel level is what most designers would consider their worst nightmare. (To be clear: *don't do this.*)

And yet, design isn't done when the sketch is done. It's not completed at the whiteboard. Instead, it's usually just getting started. So how do we get design to the pixel level? How do we get to finished visual design?

Increasingly, we're seeing teams turn to design systems. Design systems are like style guides on steroids. They were an emerging species when we completed the first edition of this book but have now become an accepted best practice for digital product teams. Large organizations like Westpac (see Figure 4-8) and GE use them. Technology-native companies like MailChimp and Medium and Salesforce and countless others use them, too. Even the US Federal Government has released a design system. There are even entire two-day conferences dedicated to them. But, before we get into why design systems are having their moment, let's talk about what they are.

Figure 4-8. *The GEL design system website from Westpac*

Design Systems: What's in a Name?

Style guides. Pattern libraries. Brand guidelines. Asset libraries. There's not a lot of common language in this part of the design world, so let's take a moment to clarify our terms.

For years, large organizations created brand guidelines—comprehensive documents of brand design and usage rules for those companies. In predigital days, these guidelines were documents, sometimes a few pages, but frequently large, comprehensive bound volumes. As the world moved online, these books sometimes moved onto the Web as PDF documents, web pages, or even wikis.

At the same time, publishers and publications often maintained style guides that covered rules of writing and content presentation. College students in the United States are familiar with the comforting strictness of *The Chicago Manual of Style*, The *MLA Style Manual and Guide to Scholarly Publishing*, and others.

The computing world's version of a style guide is exemplified by Apple's famous Human Interface Guidelines (HIG). The HIG is a comprehensive document that explains every component in Apple's operating system, provides rules for using the components, and contains examples that demonstrate proper use of the components.

Finally, developers are familiar with *asset libraries*. These collections of reusable code elements are intended to make the developer's job easier by providing tested, reusable code that's easy to download from an always-current *code repository*.

As with many ideas in the digital world, digital design systems (which we'll call design systems for the sake of brevity) are a kind of mash up of all of these ideas. A good design system contains comprehensive documentation of the elements of a design, rules and examples that govern the use of these elements, and crucially, *contains the code and other assets that actually implement the design.*

In practice, a design system functions as a single source of truth for the presentation layer of a product. Teams can sketch at the whiteboard and then quickly use the elements found in the design system to assemble a prototype or production-ready frontend.

The Value of Design Systems

Design systems are a powerful enabler of Lean UX. They allow the visual and microinteraction details of a design to be developed and maintained in parallel with the other decisions a team makes. So decisions like screen structure, process flow, information hierarchy—things that can be worked out at the whiteboard—can be handled by the right group of teammates, whereas things like color, type, and spacing can be handled by another (very likely overlapping) group of folks.

This has a couple of big benefits for teams:

- It allows the team to design faster, because they're not reinventing the wheel every time they design a screen.
- It allows the team to prototype faster, because frontend developers are working from a kit of parts—they don't need to recreate the elements of a solution each time, they can just go get the appropriate pieces out of the design system.

It also has some big benefits for organizations:

Increased consistency

A good design system is easy for developers to use. So they are more likely to use parts that they find in the design system, and less likely to "roll their own." This means a greater likelihood that their work will adhere to brand standards.

Increased quality

By centralizing the design and creation of user-facing elements, you can take advantage of the work of a few highly trained and highly specialized designers and UI developers. Their high-quality work can be implemented by other less-specialized developers in the organization to produce top-notch results.

Lower costs

A good design system is not free. It requires investment to build it and staff to maintain it. But over time, it pays for itself by providing tools and frameworks that make the users of the system—the other developers in the organization—more efficient and more productive. It allows new designers to come up to speed more quickly, for example, because it documents all of the frontend conventions used in an app. Similarly, it allows new developers to come up to speed more quickly, because the basic building blocks of their work are available in an easy-to-use framework.

Case Study: GE Design System

In 2012, GE opened GE Software in San Ramon, California. This new "Center of Excellence" (CoE) was designed to help GE improve its software game. A few years earlier, a strategic review helped the company to see just how central software had become to their business—measured in lines of code, GE was something like the 17th largest software company in the world. And yet they felt they were not treating software development with the focus it deserved.

San Ramon included a new team at GE: the GE Software User Experience Team. This small team at the heart of a giant company created their first design system in 2013 in order to scale the impact they could have. Indeed, with fewer than 50 designers to collaborate with more than 14,000 developers (inside an organization of more than 300,000 people), there was no way that this startup design team could grow quickly enough to have a meaningful effect at GE.

The team's first design system, called IIDS, for the Industrial Internet Design System, was designed by a group of internal designers with the help of a small team from Frog Design, one of the leading design firms in the world. The team built the system on top of Bootstrap, the HTML/CSS framework created by Twitter. It proved incredibly successful. Within a few years it had been downloaded by internal developers more than 11,000 times and had been used to create hundreds of applications. It helped software teams across the company produce better looking, more consistent applications. And, perhaps just as important, it created a huge amount of visibility for the software team and the UX team at San Ramon.

With that success came some problems. To be sure, simply having a good UI kit doesn't mean that a team can produce a well-designed product. Design systems don't solve every design problem. And Bootstrap was showing its limits as a platform choice. It had helped the team achieve their first objectives: get something out quickly, provide broad coverage of UI elements, and create wide adoption by being easier to use than "roll-your-own" solutions. But Bootstrap was hard to maintain and update and was just too big for most needs.

In 2015, GE Software, having had great success as an internal service bureau, morphed into GE Digital, a revenue-generating business in its own right. Their first product was called Predix (Figure 4-9), a platform on top of which developers inside and outside of GE can build software for industrial applications. And with this change of strategy, the team realized they needed to rethink their design system. Whereas earlier the goal had been to provide broad coverage and broad adoption, the new design system would be driven by new needs: it needed to enable great Predix applications, which was a more focused problem than before. It needed to *limit* the number of UI choices rather than supporting every possible UI widget. It still needed to be easy to adopt and use—it was now intended for use by GE customers—but now it was imperative that it be easy to maintain, as well.

The design system team had by this time grown to about 15 people and included design technologists (frontend developers who are passionate about both design and code), interaction designers, graphic designers, a technical writer, and a product owner.

Figure 4-9. *The GE Predix Design System*

The team chose to move the design system to a new technology platform. No longer based on Bootstrap, the system has instead been created with Polymer, a JavaScript framework that allows the team to implement Web Components. Web Components has emerged in the last few years as a way to enable more mature frontend development practices.

To create the new design system, the team spent nearly six months prototyping. Significantly, the team did not work in isolation. Instead, they paired with one of the application teams, and thus were designing components to meet the needs of their users—in this case the designers and developers working on the application teams. This point is really important. Collaborative design takes many forms. Sometimes it means designing with your cross-functional team. Sometimes it means designing with your end users. In this instance, it was a hybrid: designing with a cross-functional team of designers and developers *who actually are* your users.

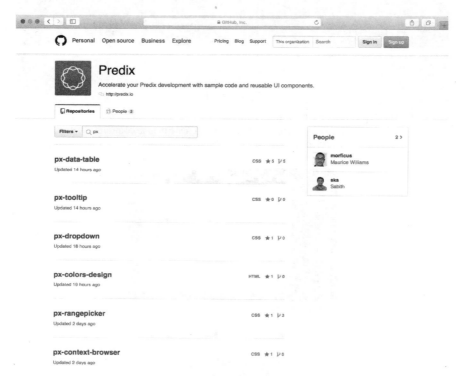

Figure 4-10. *The GE Predix Design System on GitHub*

Creating a Design System

As the GE story illustrates, there's more than one way to create a design system, and the choices you and your team make should be driven by the goals you have for the work and capabilities at your disposal. GE is a company with a large enough budget to hire excellent consultants to get the effort started, and the resources to create and dedicate a team to the effort. Is that realistic for your organization? And what goals must your design system support? Is widespread adoption important? Do you need broad coverage from day one or can you build the system over time? All of these questions will drive the approach you take. With that in mind though, here are some common themes to consider as you create your own design system.

Characteristics of successful design systems and style guides

Whether you are creating a full-blown design system or a more limited style guide, consider these important characteristics:

It takes into account audience needs
> Remember that the audience for your style guide is the entire product team. Designers, developers, QA people, will all rely on the design system for their work. Include them on the team that creates the system and make sure the contents of the system reflect their needs.

Continual improvement
> Design systems must be considered living documents. They must be a single source of truth for your organization. As your product evolves, so too must your design system. The design system should be malleable enough to add updates easily, and you must have a clear process for making these updates.

There is clear ownership
> Assign an owner to the design system. This could be a dedicated team with a product owner, an editor, or curator who works with content creators, or simply a single responsible person, but it needs to be clear who is responsible for keeping the design system up-to-date. If this becomes a burdensome responsibility, consider rotating this role on a regular basis every three months.

The system is actionable
> Your design system is not just a library or museum for user interface elements. It should be a "widget factory" that can produce any interface element on demand. As each new element is added to the system, make it available for download in whatever formats your team will need. Ensure that not only the code is available but the graphical and wireframe assets, as well. This allows every designer to have a full palette of interface elements with which to create prototypes at any given time.

The system is accessible
> Accessibility means that the design system is available to everyone in your organization. Accessible design systems are:

> *Easily found*
>> Use a memorable URL and ensure that everyone is aware of it.

Easily distributed
> Ensure that your teams can access it at their convenience (in the office, out of the office, on mobile devices, etc.).

Easy to search
> A comprehensive and accurate search of the design system greatly increases its usage.

Easy to use
> Treat this as you would any other design project. If it's not usable, it will go unused very quickly.

What goes into a design system?

If it's made of pixels, it goes into the design system. All interaction design elements should be defined and added to the design system. Use design patterns that work well in your existing product as the baseline of your design system. Form fields, labels, drop-down menus, radio button placement and behavior, Ajax and jQuery events, buttons—all of these should be included in the design system, as is illustrated in Figure 4-11, which shows the system for Salesforce.

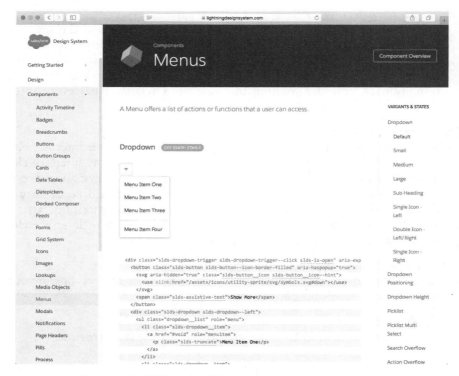

Figure 4-11. *If it's made of pixels, it goes into the design system*

Provide three data points for each interaction design element (see Figure 4-12):

What does the element look like?
Include detail about the minimum and maximum sizes of the element, vertical and horizontal constraints, and any styling demands on the element.

Where it's usually placed on the screen
Make it clear if an element should be consistently placed in certain areas of the screen as well as any exceptions that might negate this design pattern.

When it should be used
It's imperative that your team knows when to use a drop-down menu over a radio button and other factors that would determine the selection of one UI element in place of another.

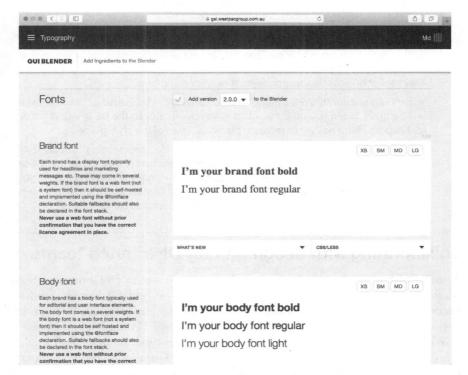

Figure 4-12. *A detail from the Westpac GEL design system*

Next, include all visual design elements. Begin with the general color palette of your product. Ensure that each primary color is available with hex values along with complementary and secondary color choices. If certain elements, like buttons, for example, have different colors based on state, include this information in the description. Other elements to include here are logos, headers, footers, grid structures, and typographical choices (i.e., which fonts to use where and at what size/weight). The same attributes of what, where, and when provided for interaction design elements should also be provided here.

Finally, you need to codify copywriting styles, as well. Capture the tone of your brand, specific words you will and won't use, grammatical choices, tolerated (and not) colloquialisms, along with button language ("OK," "Yes," "Go," etc.) and other navigation language (previous/next, more/less, and so on).

Alternatives: The Wiki-Based Style Guide

Of course, not every team will have the wherewithal to create a design system. For teams that can't justify the effort, you can still get a lot of value out of a wiki-based style guide. Here's why:

- Wikis are familiar places for developers. This means that getting your teammates in engineering to participate in this tool will not involve forcing them to learn a new tool or one that was purpose-built only for designers.

- Wikis keep revision histories (good ones do anyway). This is crucial because there will be times when you might want to roll back updates to the UI. Revision histories keep you from having to recreate previous states of the style guide.

- Wikis keep track of who changed what and provide commenting functionality. This is ideal for keeping a trail of what decisions were made, who made them, and what the rationale and even the discussion were for making that change. As you onboard new team members, this type of historical capture can bring them up to speed much faster, as well. In other words, wikis are your documentation.

Collaborating with Geographically Distributed Teams

Physical distance is one of the biggest challenges to strong collaboration. Some of the methods we've discussed in this chapter—especially Design Studio—become more difficult when a team isn't all in the same location. But you still find ways to collaborate. Tools such as Skype, Google Hangouts, and Slack can provide teams with the means to collaborate in real time. Google Docs (including Google Draw) and purpose-built services like Mural.com allow teammates to collaborate on a document at the same time. Trello and wikis make it possible for teams to track information together. And a phone with a camera can make it easy to quickly share photos in an ad hoc way. All these tools can make cross-time-zone collaboration more effective and can help teams to feel virtually connected for long periods of time during the day.

Collaborative Design Sessions with Distributed Teams

Working on a geographically distributed team can make collaborative design more difficult. The benefits of collaboration are worth making the extra effort it takes to overcome the challenge of distance. Let's take a look at how one team we worked with overcame a continent-wide separation and designed solutions together.

This team was spread into two groups in two cities: the product and user experience team was in New York and the development team was in Vancouver. Our goal was to run a Design Studio and affinity mapping session with the entire team.

Set up

We asked the two groups to gather in their individual conference rooms with their own laptops. Each conference room had a Mac in it with a location-specific Skype account (that is, it wasn't a specific individual's account—it was an "office" account). The two offices connected to each other via their office Skype accounts so that we could see each other as a group. This visual element was critical because it was the closest we could get to physically being in the same room.

We prepared a very brief (roughly 10 slides) setup presentation that explained the problem statement we were tackling. It included customer testimonials and data, and a very brief recap of our customers' needs. The presentation also included the constraints of the solution space.

Priming the pump with affinity mapping

We kicked things off with an affinity mapping exercise. Typically, these are done by using sticky notes and a whiteboard. In this case, we used a shared Google Doc spreadsheet to conduct the exercise, as shown in Figure 4-13. We asked everyone in both offices to sign in to the shared spreadsheet. The spreadsheet itself had a column labeled for each person. Google Docs allows multiple editors to work in the same document. For this meeting, we had eight team members in the document at the same time!

We asked the team to come up with as many ideas as they could think of to solve the problem we presented. Each team member wrote one idea per cell in the column marked with that individual's name. We gave the team five minutes to generate as many ideas as they could.

Next, to make sure everyone in each location was aware of all of the proposals, we asked the team members to read their ideas to the distributed team. Some ideas went by quickly, whereas others generated more discussion.

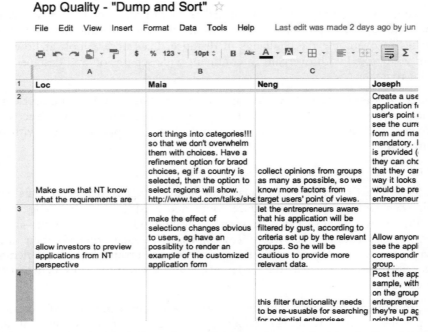

Figure 4-13. *Using Google Sheets for an affinity mapping session with a distributed team*

To simulate affinity grouping in the shared spreadsheet, one member of the team, serving as a facilitator, began a second sheet in the document using a personal laptop. The facilitator created some initial column headers in the second sheet that reflected recurring themes that emerged from discussion.

Then, we asked the team to group the ideas under the themes. Everyone moved their own ideas into the theme sheet, and people were free to add new themes if they felt their ideas didn't fit into any of the existing themes. At the end of this process, we had created a spreadsheet filled with ideas that were sorted into themes. Some themes had just a pair of ideas; others had as many as eight.

Design Studio with remote teams

To set up for the next step, a Design Studio session, we tried to mimic a colocated version of the activity as much as possible. We provided paper and pens at each location. We created a dual-monitor setup in each conference room so that each room would be able to see the sketches on one monitor while still being able to see their teammates via Skype on the second monitor, as shown in Figure 4-14. We asked each team to use a phone to photograph their sketches and email them to everyone else. This helped connect the dialog and the artifact to the conversation.

Figure 4-14. *Dual monitor setup during remote Design Studio*

After that initial setup, we were able to proceed with the Design Studio process as normal. Team members were able to present their ideas to both rooms and to receive trans-continental critique. The two teams were able to refine their ideas together and were eventually able to converge on one idea to take forward.

Making Collaboration Work

Not every team will find that collaboration comes easily. Most of us begin our careers by developing our individual technical skills as designers, developers, and so on. And in many organizations, collaboration across disciplines is rare. So it's no wonder that it can feel challenging.

One of the most powerful tools for improving collaboration is the Agile technique of the *retrospective* and the related practice of creating *Team Working Agreements*. Retrospectives are regularly scheduled meetings, usually held at the end of every sprint, in which the team takes an honest look back at the past sprint. They examine what went well, what went poorly, and what the team wants to improve. Usually, the team will select a few things to work on for the next sprint. We can think of no more powerful tool for improving collaboration than the regular practice of effective retrospectives.

A *Team Working Agreement* is a document that serves as a partner to the retrospective. It keeps track of how the team has chosen to work together. It's a self-created, continuously updated rule book that the team agrees to follow. At each retrospective, the team should check in with their Working Agreement to see if they're still following it and if they need to update it to include new agreements or remove old ones that no longer make sense.

Here's an outline for what you should consider covering in your Team Working Agreements (we've made a copy of our favorite template available online at *http://leanuxbook.com/links*):

Process overview
> What kind of process are we using? Agile? If so, what flavor? How long are our iterations?

Ceremonies
> What rituals will the team observe? For example, when is stand-up each day? When do we hold planning meetings and demos?

Communication/Tools
> What systems will we use to communicate and document our work? What is our project management tool? Where do we keep our assets?

Working hours
> Who works where? When are folks in the office? If we're in different locations, what accommodations will we make for time-zone differences?

Requirements and design
> How do we handle requirements definition, story writing, and prioritization? When is a story ready for design? When is a design ready to be broken into stories?

Development
> What practices have we settled on? Do we use pair programming? What testing style will we use? What methods will we use for source control?

Work-in-progress limits
> What is our backlog and icebox size? What WIP limits exist in various stages of our process?

Deployment
> What is our release cadence? How do we do story acceptance?

And, any additional agreements.

Wrapping Up

Collaborative design (Figure 4-15) is an evolution of the UX design process. In this chapter, we discussed how opening up the design process brings the entire team deeper into the project. We talked about how the low-fidelity drawings created in Design Studio sessions can help teams generate many ideas and then converge on a set that the entire team can get behind. We showed you practical techniques you can use to create shared understanding—the fundamental currency of Lean UX. Using tools like design systems, style guides, collaborative design sessions, Design Studio, and simple conversation, your team can build a shared understanding that allows them to move forward at a much faster pace than in traditional environments.

Figure 4-15. *A team using collaborative design techniques*

Now that we have all of our assumptions declared and our design hypotheses created, we can begin the learning process. In the next chapter, we cover the Minimum Viable Product and how to use it to plan experiments. We use those experiments to test the validity of our assumptions and decide how to move forward with our project.

CHAPTER 5

Minimum Viable Products and Prototypes

*All life is an experiment. The more
experiments you make, the better.*
—Ralph Waldo Emerson

With the parts of your hypothesis now defined, you're ready to determine which product ideas are valid and which ones you should discard. In this chapter, we discuss the *Minimum Viable Product* (MVP) and its relationship to Lean UX.

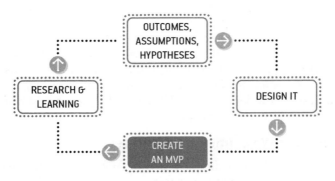

Figure 5-1. *Lean UX process*

Lean UX makes heavy use of the notion of MVP. MVPs help us test our assumptions—*will this tactic achieve the desired outcome?*—while minimizing the work we put into unproven ideas. The sooner we can find which features are worth investing in, the sooner we can focus our limited resources on the best solutions to our business problems. This is an important part of how Lean UX minimizes waste.

In addition, we cover the following:

- What is an MVP anyway? We'll resolve the confusion about what the phrase means.
- Creating an MVP. We'll share a set of guidelines for creating MVPs.
- Examples of MVPs. We'll share some inspiration and models that you can use in different situations.
- We'll talk about how to create prototypes for Lean UX, and what you'll need to consider when selecting a prototyping approach.

What Is an MVP Anyway?

If you ask a room full of technology professionals the question, "What is an MVP?" you're likely to hear a lengthy and diverse list that includes such gems as the ones that follow:

- "It's the fastest thing we can get out the door that still works."
- "It's whatever the client says it is."
- "It's the minimum set of features that allow us to say 'it works.'"
- "It's Phase 1." (and we all know about the likelihood of Phase 2)

The phrase MVP has caused a lot of confusion in its short life. The problem is that it gets used in two different ways. Sometimes, teams create an MVP primarily to *learn something*. They're not concerned with delivering value to the market—they're just trying to figure out what the market wants. In other cases, teams create a small version of a product or a feature because they want to start *delivering value* to the market as quickly as possible. In this second case, if you design and deploy the MVP correctly, you should also be able to learn from it, even if that's not the primary focus.

Example: Should We Launch a Newsletter?

Let's take, for example, a medium-sized company we consulted with recently. They were exploring new marketing tactics and wanted to launch a monthly newsletter. Newsletter creation is no small task. You need to prepare a content strategy, editorial calendar, layout and design, as well as an ongoing marketing and distribution strategy. You need writers and editors to work on it. All in all, it was a big expenditure for the company to undertake. The team decided to treat this newsletter idea as a hypothesis.

The team asked themselves: *What's the most important thing we need to know first?* The answer: *Was there enough customer demand for a newsletter to justify the effort?* The MVP the company used to test the idea was a sign-up form on their current website. The sign-up form promoted the newsletter and asked for a customer's email address. This approach wouldn't deliver any value to the customer—yet. Instead, the goal was to measure demand and build insight on what value proposition and language drove sign-ups. The team felt that these tests would give them enough information to make a good decision about whether to proceed.

The team spent half a day designing and coding the form and was able to launch it that same afternoon. The team knew that their site received a significant amount of traffic each day: they would be able to learn very quickly if there was interest in the newsletter.

At this point, the team made no effort to design or build the actual newsletter. After the team had gathered enough data from their first experiment, and *if* the data showed that its customers wanted the newsletter, the team would move on to their next MVP, one that would begin to deliver value and create deeper learning around the type of content, presentation format, frequency, social distribution, and the other things they would need to learn to create a good newsletter. The team planned to continue experimenting with MVP versions of the newsletter—each one improving on its predecessor—that would provide more and different types of content and design, and ultimately deliver the business benefit they were seeking.

Creating an MVP

When it comes to creating an MVP, the first question is always *what is the most important thing we need to learn next?* In most cases, the answer to that will either be a question of *value* or a question of *implementation*.

Your prioritized list of hypotheses has given you several paths to explore. As a team, discuss the first hypothesis in your list with the following framework:

- What's the most important thing we need to learn first (or next) about this hypothesis? In other words, what's the biggest risk currently associated with this approach?

- What's the least amount of work we can do to learn that? This isn't lazy: it's Lean. There's no reason to do any more work than you need to in order to determine your next step.

The answer to the second question is your MVP. You will use your MVP to run experiments and the outcome of those experiments will inform you as to whether your hypothesis was correct. These experiments should provide you with enough evidence to decide whether the direction you are exploring should be pursued, refined, or abandoned.

Creating an MVP to Understand Value

Here are some guidelines to follow if you're trying to understand the value of your idea:

Get to the point
Regardless of the MVP method you choose to use, focus your time distilling your idea to its core value proposition and present that to your customers. The things that surround your idea (things like navigation, logins, and password retrieval flows) will be irrelevant if your idea itself has no value to your target audience. Leave that stuff for later.

Use a clear call to action
You will know people value your solution when they demonstrate intent to use it or, gasp, pay for it. Giving people a way to opt in to or sign up for a service is a great way to know if they're interested and whether they'd actually give you money for it.

Prioritize ruthlessly
Ideas, like artifacts, are transient. Let the best ones prove themselves and don't hold onto invalidated ideas just because you like them. As designers ourselves, we know that this one is particularly difficult to practice. Designers tend to be optimists and often, we believe our solutions, whether we worked on them for five minutes or five months, are well-crafted and properly thought out. Remember, if the results of your experiment disagree with your design, it's wrong.

Stay agile
Learnings will come in quickly; make sure you're working in a medium or tool that allows you to make updates easily.

Don't reinvent the wheel
Lots of the mechanisms and systems that you need to test your ideas already exist. Consider how you could use email, SMS, chat apps, Facebook Groups, eBay storefronts, discussion forums, and other existing tools to get the learning you're seeking.

Measure behavior
Build MVPs with which you can observe and measure what people do. This lets you bypass what people say they (will) do in favor of what they actually do. In digital product design, behavior trumps opinion.

Talk to your users

Measuring behavior tells you "what" people did with your MVP. Without knowing "why" they behaved that way, iterating your MVP is an act of random design. Try to capture conversations from both those who converted as well as those who didn't.

Creating an MVP to Understand Implementation

Here are some guidelines to follow if you're trying to understand the implementation you're considering launching to your customers:

Be functional

Some level of integration with the rest of your application must be in place to create a realistic usage scenario. Creating your new workflow in the context of the existing functionality is important here.

Integrate with existing analytics

Measuring the performance of your MVP must be done within the context of existing product workflows. This will help you to understand the numbers you're seeing.

Be consistent with the rest of the application

To minimize any biases toward the new functionality, design your MVP to fit with your current look, feel, and brand. (This is where your Design System provides a ton of efficiency.)

Some Final Guidelines for Creating MVPs

MVPs might seem simple, but in practice but can prove challenging. Like most skills, the more you practice, the better you become at doing it. In the meantime, here are some guidelines to building valuable MVPs:

It's not easy to be pure

You'll find that it's not always possible to test only one thing at a time: you're often trying to learn whether your idea has value *and* determine implementation details at the same time. Although it's better to separate these processes, keeping the aforementioned guidelines in mind as you plan your MVPs will help you to navigate the trade-offs and compromises you're going to have to make.

Be clear about your learning goals

Make sure that you know what you're trying to learn, and make sure you are clear about what data you need to collect to learn. It's a bad feeling to launch an experiment only to discover you haven't instrumented correctly, and are failing to capture some important data.

Go small

Regardless of your desired outcome, build the smallest MVP possible. Remember that it is a tool for learning. You will be iterating. You will be modifying it. You might very well be throwing it away entirely.

You don't necessarily need code

In many cases, your MVP won't involve any code at all. Instead you will rely on many of the UX designer's existing tools: sketching, prototyping, copywriting, and visual design.

The Truth Curve

The amount of effort you put into your MVP should be proportional to the amount of evidence you have that your idea is a good one. That's the point of the chart (Figure 5-2) created by Giff Constable (http://giffconstable.com/2013/06/the-truth-curve/). The X axis shows the level of investment you should put into your MVP. The Y axis shows the amount of market-based evidence you have about your idea. The more evidence you have, the higher the fidelity and complexity of your MVP can be. (You'll need the extra effort, because what you need to learn becomes more complex.) The less evidence you have, the less effort you want to put into your MVP. Remember the key question: *What's the smallest thing that you can do to learn the next most important thing?* Anything more than that is waste.

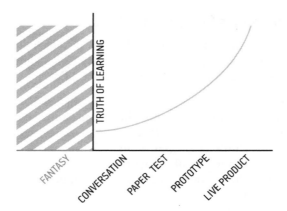

Figure 5-2. *The Truth Curve is a useful reminder that learning is continuous and increased investment is only warranted when the facts dictate it*

Examples of MVPs

Let's take a look at a few different types of MVPs that are in common use:

Landing page test

This type of MVP helps a team determine demand for their product. It involves creating a marketing page with a clear value proposition, a call to action, and a way to measure conversion. Teams must drive relevant traffic to this landing page to get a large enough sample size for the results to be useful. They can do this either by diverting traffic from existing workflows or utilizing online advertising.

Positive results from landing page tests are clear, but negative results can be difficult to interpret. If no one "converts," it doesn't necessarily mean your idea has no value. It could just mean that you're not telling a compelling story. The good news is that landing page tests are cheap and can be iterated very quickly. In fact, there are products and services out there now such as Unbounce and LaunchRocket that are set up strictly for this type of learning. If you think about it, Kickstarter (and other crowdfunding sites) are full of landing page MVPs, as demonstrated in Figure 5-3. The people who list products on those sites are looking for validation (in the form of financial backing) that they should invest in actually building their proposed ideas.

Feature fake (aka the button to nowhere)

Sometimes, the cost of implementing a feature is very high. In these cases, it is cheaper and faster to learn about the value of the idea to create *the appearance of the feature* where none actually exists. HTML buttons, calls to action, and other prompts and links provide the illusion to your customer that a feature exists. Upon clicking or tapping the link, the user is notified that the feature is "coming soon" and that he will be alerted when this has happened. They're like mini-landing pages, in that they exist to measure interest. Feature fakes should be used sparingly and taken down as soon as a success threshold has been reached. If you feel they might negatively affect your relationship with your customer, you can make it right by offering those that found your mousetrap a gift card or some other kind of compensation. And they're not right for every business or every context.

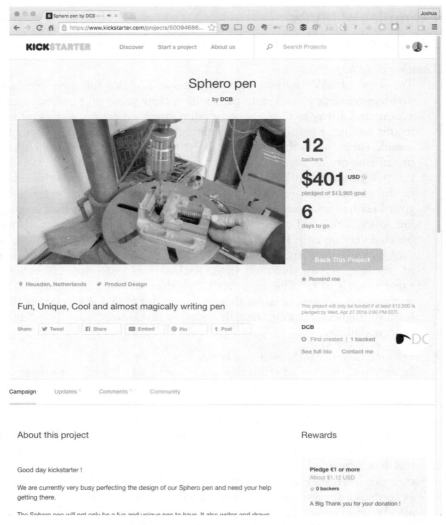

Figure 5-3. *An example of a Kickstarter page*

Figure 5-4 shows a feature fake that Flickr used. In this case, they offered a button labeled "Use as screensaver" that was ostensibly meant for the user to specify a photo album as the screensaver for their device. When users clicked the button, though, they were greeted by the screen shown in Figure 5-5. Flickr used this to gather evidence that a customer would like this feature. By measuring click rates, they could assess demand for this feature before they built it.

Figure 5-4. *An example of a feature fake found in Flickr's Apple TV app*

Figure 5-5. *The screen that appears after clicking the feature-fake button*

Figure 5-6 presents another feature-fake example. Here, MapMyRun offered the opportunity to take and upload photos while jogging using two modal overlays. No feature existed until they got an indication that a) people wanted this feature, and b) how much they'd be willing to pay for it.

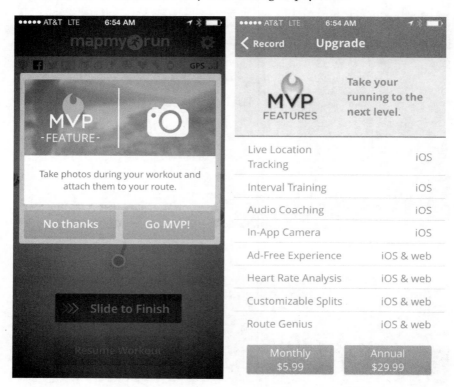

Figure 5-6. *Another example of a feature fake, this one on the MapMyRun website*

Wizard of Oz

After you've proven demand for your idea, a Wizard of Oz MVP can help you to figure out the mechanics of your product. This type of MVP looks like a fully functioning digital service to the user. Behind the scenes though, the data and communication with the initial set of users is handled manually by humans. For example, the team at Amazon behind the Echo ran a Wizard of Oz MVP as part of their initial testing to understand the types of queries people would ask and how quickly they would expect a response. In one room, a user would ask "Alexa" questions and in another room, a human typed queries into Google, got answers, and replied back. The test users were not aware that they were not using software. The rest of the team was able to observe users and understand how they would use this new product—before significant engineering effort had been invested.

Example: Wizard of Oz MVP for Taproot Plus

In 2014, our company worked with an organization called Taproot Foundation to create an online marketplace for pro bono volunteers.

NOTE

Pro bono is when a professional donates his skills to help a worthy cause. Unlike the unskilled volunteer services many of us participate in on the weekend, pro bono service involves using your professional talents in a volunteer context.

Our client, Taproot Foundation, had been helping pro bono volunteers and nonprofit organizations find each other for years, but they had always delivered this matching service "by hand," through phone calls, emails, and in-person meetings. Now, they wanted to bring that process online: they wanted to create a website that would act as a two-sided marketplace for pro bono volunteers and the organizations that could benefit from their services.

As we started the project, we faced a big set of questions: how should the matching process work? Should the volunteers advertise their services? Should the organizations advertise their projects? What would work better? And after the parties found each other on the website, how should they get started with the project? How should the organizations communicate their needs? How should the volunteers scope the work? Even little details were big questions: how should the parties schedule their first phone call?

We decided this was a perfect time to create a Wizard of Oz MVP. We built a simple website, handcoding just the few static pages that we needed to make it look like we were open for business. We began with about a dozen pages in all: one index page, and then a page for each of the 12 pilot projects we had lined up. Behind the scenes, we had a community manager assemble a list of potential volunteers, and we emailed them, sending them a call to action and a link to our new site. To maintain the illusion that we had a running system, we made sure the email looked like it came from our new system, not from the community manager.

When volunteers clicked the link in the email, they saw our Wizard of Oz site (Figure 5-7). When they used the site to apply for a volunteer opportunity, it looked to them like they were interacting with the system, but behind the scenes, it simply emailed the community manager and team. We tracked all of our interactions in a simple Trello board (Figure 5-8), which served as our "database."

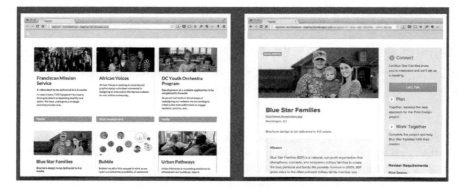

Figure 5-7. *The Wizard of Oz site for Taproot Foundation*

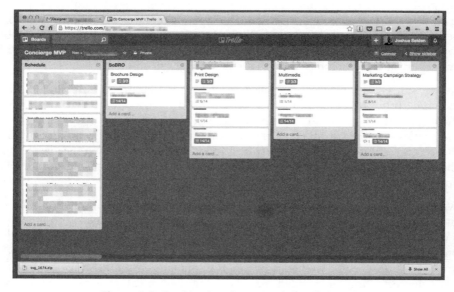

Figure 5-8. *Our "database" was simply a Trello board*

We operated the system this way for a few months, gradually learning from our interactions, updating our business processes, and adding automation and other updates to the website as we learned. Eventually, we added a real functional backend, eliminating much of the "man behind the curtain" aspect of the site. We also updated the visual style, applying some mature graphic design polish (Figure 5-9)—after we had learned enough to understand how to communicate our brand.

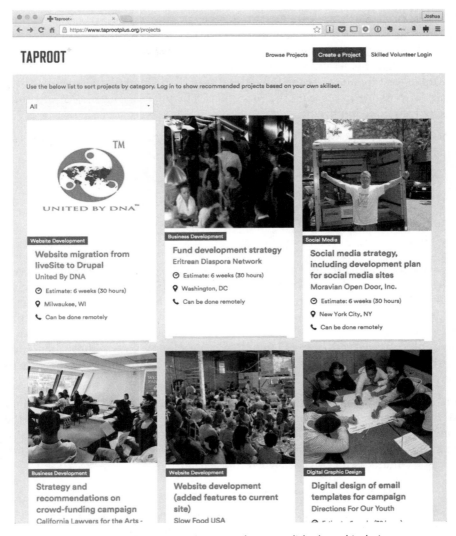

Figure 5-9. *The Taproot Plus site with more polished graphic design*

By using a Wizard of Oz approach, we were able to pilot the high-risk parts of the design—the design of the business processes—learn as we went along, and eliminate the risk of spending lots of time and money designing and building the wrong thing.

Prototyping

One of the most effective ways to create MVPs is by prototyping the experience. A prototype is an approximation of an experience that allows you to simulate what it is like to use the product or service in question. It needs to be clickable (or tappable). At the same time, your goal should be to spend as little effort as possible in creating the prototype. This makes your choice of prototyping technique important.

Choosing which technique to use for your prototype depends on several factors:

- Who will be interacting with it?
- What you hope to learn
- What you already know to be true
- How much time you have to create it

It's critical to define the intended audience for your prototype. This allows you to create the smallest possible prototype that will generate meaningful feedback from this audience. For example, if you're using the prototype primarily to demo ideas to software engineers on your team, you can largely omit primary areas of the product that aren't being affected by the new experience—the global navigation, for example. Your developers know those items are there and that they're not changing, so you don't need to illustrate these items for them.

Stakeholders, often less familiar with their own product than they'll ever admit to, will likely need a greater level of fidelity in the prototype to truly grasp the concept. To meet the various needs of these disparate audiences, your prototyping toolkit should be fairly broad. Let's take a look at the different prototyping techniques and consider when to use each.

------ **NOTE** ------

The list of prototyping tools changes regularly, with new, exciting tools emerging frequently. Trying to capture a comprehensive and up-do-date list in a book is difficult. If you've read the first edition of this book, you'll know how quickly such a list goes out of date. Instead of listing out specific tools here, we've created a list, which is available at *http://www.leanuxbook.com/links*.

Paper Prototypes

Made of the most accessible components—paper, pens, and tape—paper prototypes give you the ability to simulate experiences in a quick, crafty, fun way. No digital investment is necessary. Using tactics like flaps to show and hide different states on a page or even creating a "window" for a slideshow of images to move through, you can begin to give the team a sense of how the product should function. You'll be able to get an immediate sense of what is available in the experience and what is missing. Paper prototyping can give you a sense of how the workflow is starting to coalesce around the interface elements you've assembled. This method is especially helpful with touch interfaces that require the user to manipulate elements on a screen.

Pros

- Can be created in an hour
- Easily arranged and rearranged
- Cheap and easy to throw away if you're wrong
- Can be assembled with materials already found in the office
- Fun activity that many people enjoy

Cons

- Rapid iteration and duplication of the prototype can become time-consuming and tedious.
- The simulation is very artificial, because you're not using the actual input mechanisms (mouse, track-pad, keyboard, touch screen, etc.).
- Feedback is limited to the high-level structure, information architecture, and flow of the product.
- Only useful with limited audience.

Low-Fidelity On-Screen Mockups

Creating a low-fidelity clickable on-screen experience—clickable wireframes, for example—lets you take a prototype to the next level of fidelity. Your investment in pixels provides a bit more realistic feel to the workflow. Test participants and team members use digital input mechanisms to interact with the prototype. This lets you get better insight and feedback about the way they will interact with the product at the level of the click, tap, or gesture.

Pros

- Provide a good sense of the length of workflow
- Reveal major obstacles to primary task completion
- Allow assessment of findability of core elements

- Can be used to quickly wire up "something clickable" to get your team learning from your existing assets instead of forcing the creation of new ones

Cons

- Most people who will interact with these assets are savvy enough to recognize an unfinished product.
- More attention than normal is paid to labeling and copy.

Middle- and High-Fidelity On-Screen Prototypes

Middle- and high-fidelity prototypes have significantly more detail than wireframe-based prototypes. You'll use these to demonstrate and test designs that are fleshed out with a level of interaction, visual design, and content that is similar to (or indistinguishable from) the final product experience. The level of interactivity that you can create at this level varies from tool to tool; however, most tools in this category will allow you to represent pixel-perfect simulations of the final experience. You will be able to create interface elements like form fields and drop-down menus that work and form buttons that simulate submit actions. Some tools allow logical branching and basic data operations. Many allow some types of minor animations, transitions, and state changes.

Pros

- Produce prototypes that are high quality and realistic
- Visual design and brand elements can be tested
- Workflow and user interface interactions can be assessed

Cons

- Interactivity is still more limited than fully native prototypes.
- Users typically can't interact with real data, so there is a limit to the types of product interactions you can simulate.
- Depending on the tool, it can be time-consuming to create and maintain these prototypes. It often creates duplicate effort to maintain a high-fidelity prototype and keep it in sync with the actual product.

Coded and Live-Data Prototypes

Coded prototypes offer up the highest level of fidelity for simulated experiences. For all intents and purposes, people interacting with this type of prototype should not be able to distinguish it from the final product unless they bump up against the limits of its scope (i.e., they click a link to a page that was not prototyped). Coded prototypes typically exist in the native environment (the browser, the OS, on the device, etc.) and make use of all of the expected interactive elements. Buttons, drop-down menus, and form fields all function as the user would expect. They take input from the mouse, keyboard, and screen. They create as natural an interaction pattern as possible for the prototype's evaluators.

In terms of prototyping with data, there are two levels of fidelity here: *hardcoded* (or static data) and *live data*. The hardcoded prototypes look and function like the end product but don't handle real data input, processing, or output. They are still just simulations, and typically illustrate a few predefined scenarios. The live-data prototypes will connect with real data, process user input, and show appropriate data outputs. These are often deployed to real customers and offer a level of realism to customers and insight into the customers' use of the prototype that are not available from hardcoded prototypes. You also can use them when A/B testing (that is, comparing two versions of a feature to see which performs better) certain features or changes to the current workflow.

Pros

- Potential to reuse code for production
- The most realistic simulation to create
- Can be generated from existing code assets

Cons

- The team can become bogged down in debating the finer points of the prototype.
- Time-consuming to create working code that delivers the desired experience.
- It's tempting to perfect the code before releasing to customers.
- Updating and iterating can take a lot of time.

What Should Go into My Prototype?

You've picked the tool to create your MVP and are ready to begin. There is no need to prototype the entire product experience. Focus on the core workflows that let you test your hypothesis.

Focusing on the primary workflows when you create your MVP gives the team a sense of temporary tunnel vision (in a good way!), allowing them to focus on a specific portion of the experience and assess its validity and efficacy.

Demos and Previews

You might have developed your MVP with a focus on just one kind of user, or just one segment of your customer base, but you can learn a lot by sharing your work with your colleagues. Test your prototyped MVP with your team-mates, stakeholders, and members of other teams. Take it to the lunch area and share it with some colleagues who work on different projects. Ensure that, internally, people are providing the team with insights into how well it works, how they'll use it, and if it's worth investing in further. Let stakeholders click through it and give you their insights and thoughts.

If your team has a demo day (and if they don't, they should) bring the proto-type there to show progress on the project. The more exposure the MVP receives, the more insight you'll have as to its validity. Next, take your proto-type to customers and potential customers. Let them click through the experi-ence and collect their feedback.

Example: Using a Prototype MVP

Let's see how one team we recently worked with used a prototype MVP. In this case study, the team was considering making a significant change to their offer-ing. We used a prototype MVP to support the research and decision-making process.

This established startup was struggling with their current product—an exclu-sive subscription-based community for group collaboration. It had been in market for a few years and had some initial traction, but adoption had reached a plateau—new users were not signing up. What's more, the product was fac-ing growing competition. Realizing that a radical change was in order, the team considered revamping their business model and opening up the product to a significantly broader market segment. Their concern was two-fold:

- Would current users accept this change; given that it would alter the exclu-sive nature of the community?
- Would the new market segment even be interested in this type of product?

The team was worried that they could take a double-hit. They feared that existing users would abandon the product and that there wouldn't be enough new users coming on board to make up for the shortfall.

We worked with the team to define our plan as a hypothesis. We laid out the new market segment and defined the core set of functionality that we wanted to offer to them. This was a subset of the ultimate vision, but it could be demonstrated in five wireframes.

We spent a week creating the wireframes using Balsamiq to ensure that our developers, marketers, and executives were committed to the new direction. We showed the wireframes to current customers, getting two rounds of customer feedback over the course of these five days, and we ended up with a clickable prototype—our MVP.

The timing for our experiment was fortuitous: there was a conference full of potential customers scheduled for the following week in Texas. The team went to the conference and walked the halls of the convention center with the prototype on our iPads.

The mockups worked great on the iPads: customers tapped, swiped, and chatted with us about the new offering. Three days later, we returned to New York City with feedback written on every sticky note and scrap of paper we could find.

We sorted the notes into groups, and some clear themes emerged. Customer feedback let us conclude that although there was merit to this new business plan, we would need further differentiation from existing products in the marketplace if we were going to succeed.

All told, we spent eight business days developing our hypotheses, creating our MVP, and getting market feedback. This put us in a great position to pivot our position and refine the product to fit our market segment more effectively.

Wrapping Up

In this chapter, we defined the Minimum Viable Product as the smallest thing you can make to learn whether your hypothesis is valid. In addition, we discussed the various forms an MVP can take and took a closer look at prototyping.

Remember that the entire point of an MVP is to learn. If you focus on what you're trying to learn and apply your team's creativity to learning quickly, you'll be well on your way to creating great MVPs.

In Chapter 6, we take a look at various types of research that you can use to make sure your designs are hitting the mark. We also take a look at how your team can make sense of all the feedback your research will generate.

CHAPTER 6

Feedback and Research

*Research is formalized curiosity. It is
poking and prying with a purpose.*
—Zora Neale Hurston

It's now time to put your Minimum Viable Product (MVP) to the test. All of
our work up to this point has been based on assumptions; now we must begin
the validation process. We use lightweight, continuous, and collaborative
research techniques to do this.

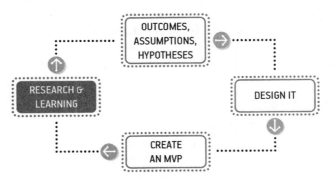

Figure 6-1. *The Lean UX cycle*

Research with users is at the heart of most approaches to User Experience
(UX) design. Too often though, teams outsource research work to specialized
research teams. And, too often, research activities take place on rare occasions
—either at the beginning of a project or at the end. Lean UX solves the prob-

lems these tactics create by making research both *continuous* and *collabora-tive*. Let's dig in to see how to do that.

In this chapter, we cover the following:

- Collaborative research techniques with which you can build shared under-standing with your team
- Continuous research techniques that you can use to build small, informal, qualitative research studies into every iteration
- How to use small units of regular research to build longitudinal research studies
- How to reconcile contradictory feedback from multiple sources
- What artifacts to test and what results you can expect from each of these tests
- How to incorporate the voice of the customer throughout the Lean UX cycle

Continuous and Collaborative Research

Lean UX takes basic UX research techniques and overlays two important ideas. First, Lean UX research is continuous. This means you build research activities into every sprint. Instead of being a costly and disruptive "big bang" process, we make it bite-sized so that we can fit it into our ongoing process. Second, Lean UX research is collaborative. This means that you don't rely on the work of specialized researchers to deliver learning to your team. Instead, research activities and responsibilities are distributed and shared across the entire team. By eliminating the handoff between researchers and team members, we increase the quality of our learning. Our goal in all of this is to create a rich *shared understanding* across the team.

Collaborative Discovery

Collaborative discovery is the process of working together as a team to test ideas in the market. It is one of the two main cross-functional techniques that create shared understanding on a Lean UX team. (Collaborative design, cov-ered in Chapter 4, is the other.) Collaborative discovery is an approach to research that gets the entire team out of the building—literally and figuratively —to meet with and learn from customers. It gives everyone on the team a chance to see how the hypotheses are tested and, most important, multiplies the number of perspectives the team can use to gather customer insight.

It's essential that you and your team conduct research together; that's why we call it *collaborative* discovery. Outsourcing research dramatically reduces its value: it wastes time, it limits team-building, and it filters the information through deliverables, handoffs, and interpretation. Don't do it.

Researchers sometimes feel uneasy about this approach. As trained professionals, they are right to point out that they have special knowledge that is important to the research process. We agree. That's why you should include a researcher on your team if you can. Just don't outsource the work to that person. Instead, use the researcher as an expert guide to help your team plan their work and lead the team through their research activities. In the same way that Lean UX encourages designers to take a more facilitative approach, Lean UX asks the same of the researcher. Use your expertise to help the team plan good research, ask good questions, and select the right methods for the job. Just don't do all the research for them.

Collaborative Discovery in the Field

Collaborative discovery is simply a way to get out into the field with your team. Here's how you do it:

- As a team, review your questions, assumptions, hypotheses, and MVPs. Decide as a team what you need to learn.
- Working as a team, decide who you'll need to speak to and observe to address your learning goals.
- Create an interview guide (see the sidebar "The Interview Guide" on page 98) that you can all use to guide your conversations.
- Break your team into research pairs, mixing up the various roles and disciplines within each pair (i.e., try not to have designers paired with designers). If you are doing this research over a number of days, try to mix up the interview pairs each day so that people have a chance to share experiences with various team members.
- Arm each pair with a version of the MVP.
- Send each team out to meet with customers/users.
- One team member interviews while the other takes notes.
- Begin with questions, conversations, and observations.
- Demonstrate the MVP later in the session, and allow the customer to interact with it.
- Collect notes as the customer provides feedback.
- When the lead interviewer is done, switch roles to give the note taker a chance to ask follow-up questions.

- At the end of the interview, ask the customer for referrals to other people who might also provide useful feedback.

The Interview Guide

To prepare for field work, create a small cheat sheet that will fit into your notebook. On your cheat sheet, write the questions and topics that you've decided to cover. This way you'll always be prepared to move the interview along.

When planning your questions, think about a sequential funnel:

- First, try to identify if the customer is in your target audience.
- Then, try to confirm any problem hypotheses you have for this segment.
- Finally, if you have a prototype or mockup with you, show this last to avoid limiting the conversation to your vision of the solution.

A Collaborative Discovery Example

A team we worked with at PayPal set out with an Axure prototype to conduct a collaborative discovery session. The team was made up of two designers, a UX researcher, four developers, and a product manager; they split into teams of two and three. They paired each developer with a nondeveloper. Before setting out, they brainstormed what they'd like to learn from their prototype and used the outcome of that session to write brief interview guides. Their product was targeted at a broad consumer market, so they decided to just head out to the local shopping malls scattered around their office. Each pair targeted a different mall. They spent two hours in the field, stopping strangers, asking them questions, and demonstrating their prototypes. To build up their skillset, they changed roles (from lead to note taker) an hour into their research.

When they reconvened, each pair read their notes to the rest of the team. Almost immediately they began to see patterns emerge, proving some of their assumptions and disproving others. Using this new information, they adjusted the design of their prototype and headed out again later that afternoon. After a full day of field research, it was clear where their idea had legs and where it needed pruning. When they began the next sprint the following day, every member of the team was working from the same baseline of clarity, having established a shared understanding by means of collaborative discovery the day before.

Continuous Learning

A critical best practice in Lean UX is building a regular cadence of customer involvement. Regularly scheduled conversations with customers minimize the time between hypothesis creation, experiment design, and user feedback—giving you the opportunity to validate your hypotheses quickly. In general, knowing you're never more than a few days away from customer feedback has a powerful effect on teams. It takes the pressure off of your decision making because you know that you're never more than a few days from getting meaningful data from the market.

Continuous Learning in the Lab: Three Users Every Thursday

Although you can create a standing schedule of fieldwork based on the aforementioned techniques, it's much easier to bring customers into the building—you just need to be a little creative to get the entire team involved.

We like to use a weekly rhythm to schedule research, as demonstrated in Figure 6-2. We call this "Three, twelve, one," because it's based on the following guidelines: *three* users; by *12* noon; *once* a week.

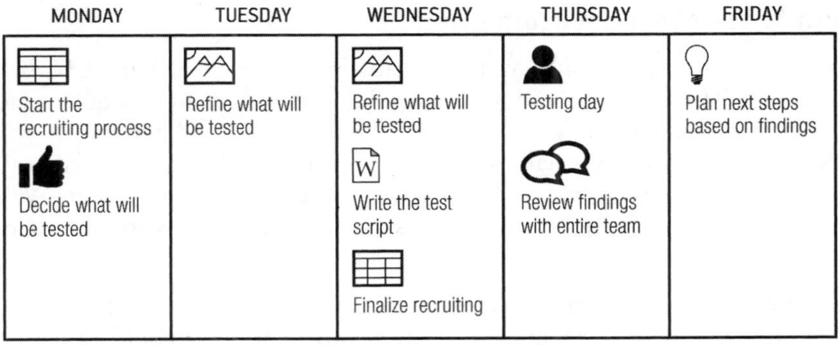

MONDAY	TUESDAY	WEDNESDAY	THURSDAY	FRIDAY
Start the recruiting process	Refine what will be tested	Refine what will be tested	Testing day	Plan next steps based on findings
Decide what will be tested		Write the test script	Review findings with entire team	
		Finalize recruiting		

Figure 6-2. *The Three, twelve, one activity calendar*

Here's how the team's activities break down:

Monday: Recruiting and planning
> Decide, as a team, what will be tested this week. Decide who you need to recruit for tests and start the recruiting process. Outsource this job if at all possible: it's very time-consuming (see the sidebar "A Word About Recruiting Participants" on page 101).

Tuesday: Refine the components of the test
> Based on what stage your MVP is in, begin refining the design, the proto-type, or the product to a point that will allow you to tell at least one complete story when your customers see it.

Wednesday: Continue refining, write the script, and finalize recruiting
> Put the final touches on your MVP. Write the test script that your moderator will follow with each participant. (Your moderator should be someone on the team if at all possible.) Finalize the recruiting and schedule for Thursday's tests.

Thursday: Test!
> Spend the morning testing your MVP with customers. Spend no more than an hour with each customer. Everyone on the team should take notes. The team should plan to watch from a separate location. Review the findings with the entire project team immediately after the last participant is done.

Friday: Plan
> Use your new insight to decide whether your hypotheses were validated and what you need to do next.

Simplify Your Test Environment

Many firms have established usability labs in-house—and it used to be you needed one. These days, you don't need a lab—all you need is a quiet place in your office and a computer with a network connection and a webcam. It used to be necessary to use specialized usability testing products to record sessions and connect remote observers. These days, you don't even need that. We routinely run tests with remote observers using nothing more exotic than Google Hangouts.

The ability to connect remote observers is a key element. It makes it possible for you to bring the test sessions to team members and stakeholders who can't be present. This has an enormous impact on collaboration because it spreads understanding of your customers deep into your organization. It's hard to overstate how powerful this is.

Who Should Watch?

The short answer is your entire team. Like almost every other aspect of Lean UX, usability testing should be a group activity. With the entire team watching the tests, absorbing the feedback, and reacting in real time, you'll find the need for subsequent debriefings reduced. The team will learn first-hand where their efforts are succeeding and failing. Nothing is more humbling (and motivating) than seeing a user struggle with the software you just built.

A Word About Recruiting Participants

Recruiting, scheduling, and confirming participants is time intensive. Save your team from this additional overhead by offloading the work to a dedicated recruiter. Some companies have hired internal recruiters to do this work, others outsource the work to a third party. In either case, the cost is worth it. The recruiter does the work and gets paid for each participant she brings in. In addition, your recruiter takes care of the screening, scheduling, and replacement of no-shows on testing day. Third-party recruiters typically charge for each participant they recruit. You'll also have to budget for whatever compensation you offer to the participants themselves.

Case Study: Three Users Every Thursday at Meetup

One company that has taken the concept of "three users every Thursday" to a new level is Meetup. Based in New York City and under the guidance of Chief Strategy Officer Andres Glusman, Meetup started with a desire to test each and every one of their new features and products.

After pricing some outsourced options, they decided to keep things in-house and take an iterative approach in their search for what they called their MVP —minimal viable *process*. Initially, Meetup tried to test with the user, moderator, and team all in the same room. They got some decent results from this approach—the company learned a lot about the products they were testing but found the test participants could feel uncomfortable with so many folks in the room.

Over time Meetup evolved to having the testing in one room with only the moderator joining the user. The rest of the team would watch the video feed from a separate conference room or at their desks. (Meetup originally used Morae to share the video. Today they use GoToMeeting.)

Meetup doesn't write testing scripts, because they're not sure what will be tested each day. Instead, product managers and designers talk with the moderator before a test to identify key assumptions and key focus areas for the test. Then, the moderator and team interact with test moderators using instant messaging to help guide the conversations with users. The team debriefs immediately after the tests are complete and are able to move forward quickly.

Meetup recruited directly from the Meetup community from day one. For participants outside of their community, the team used a third-party recruiter. Ultimately though, they decided to bring this responsibility in-house, assigning the work to the dedicated researcher the company hired to handle all testing.

The team scaled up from three users once a week to testing every day except Monday. Their core objective was to minimize the time between concept and customer feedback.

Meetup's practical *minimum viable process* orientation can be seen in their approach to mobile testing, as well. As their mobile usage numbers grew, Meetup didn't want to delay testing on mobile platforms while waiting for fancy mobile testing equipment. Instead, the company built their own—for $28 (see Figure 6-3).

Over time, Meetup scaled their minimum viable usability testing process to an impressive program. The company runs approximately 400 test sessions per year at a total cost of about $30,000 (not including staffing costs). This includes 100 percent video and notes coverage for every session. This is truly amazing when you consider that this is roughly equivalent to the cost of running one major outsourced usability study.

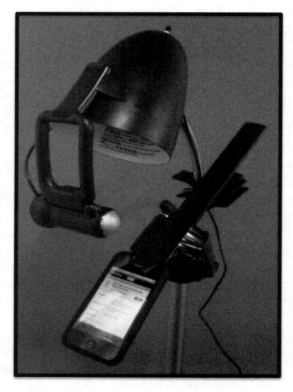

Figure 6-3. *An early version of Meetup's mobile usability testing rig (it's been refined since then)*

Making Sense of the Research: A Team Activity

Whether your team does fieldwork or labwork, research generates a lot of raw data. Making sense of this can be time-consuming and frustrating—so the process is often handed over to specialists who are asked to synthesize research findings. You shouldn't do this. Instead, work as hard as you can to make sense of the data as a team.

As soon as possible after the research sessions are over—preferably the same day, if not then the following day—gather the team together for a review session. When the team has reassembled, ask everyone to read their findings to one another. One really efficient way to do this is to transcribe the notes people read out loud onto index cards or sticky notes, and then sort the notes into themes. This process of reading, grouping, and discussing gets everyone's input out on the table and builds the shared understanding that you seek. With themes identified, you and your team can then determine the next steps for your MVP.

Confusion, Contradiction, and (Lack of) Clarity

As you and your team collect feedback from various sources and try to synthesize your findings, you will inevitably come across situations in which your data presents you with contradictions. How do you make sense of it all? Here are a couple of ways to maintain your momentum and ensure that you're maximizing your learning:

Look for patterns
> As you review the research, keep an eye out for patterns in the data. These patterns reveal multiple instances of user opinion that represent elements to explore. If something doesn't fall into a pattern, it is likely an outlier.

Place your outliers in a "parking lot"
> Tempting as it is to ignore outliers (or try to serve them in your solution), don't do it. Instead, create a parking lot or backlog. As your research progresses over time (remember: you're doing this every week), you might discover other outliers that match the pattern. Be patient.

Verify with other sources
> If you're not convinced the feedback you're seeing through one channel is valid, look for it in other channels. Are the customer support emails reflecting the same concerns as your usability studies? Is the value of your prototype echoed with customers inside and outside your office? If not, your sample might have been disproportionately skewed.

Identifying Patterns Over Time

Typical UX research programs are structured to get a conclusive answer. Typically, you will plan to do enough research to conclusively answer a question or set of questions. Lean UX research puts a priority on being continuous—which means that you are structuring your research activities very differently. Instead of running big studies, you are seeing a small number of users every week. This means that you might discover some questions remain open over a couple of weeks. The opposite effect, though, is that interesting patterns can reveal themselves over time.

For example, over the course of regular test sessions from 2008 to 2011, the team at the TheLadders watched an interesting change in their customers' attitudes over time. In 2008, when they first began meeting with job seekers on a regular basis, they would discuss various ways to communicate with employers. One of the options they proposed was SMS. In 2008, the audience, made up of high-income earners in their late 40s and early 50s, showed a strong disdain for SMS as a legitimate communication method. To them, it was something their kids did (and that perhaps they did with their kids), but it was certainly not a "proper" way to conduct a job search.

By 2011 though, SMS messages had taken off in the United States. As text messaging gained acceptance in business culture, audience attitudes began to soften. Week after week, as they sat with job seekers, they began to see opinions about SMS change. The team saw job seekers become far more likely to use SMS in a mid-career job search than they would have been just a few years earlier.

The team at TheLadders would never have recognized this as an audience-wide trend were it not for two things. First, they were speaking with a sample of their audience week in and week out. Additionally, though, the team took a systematic approach to investigating long-term trends. As part of their regular interaction with customers, they always asked a regular set of level-setting questions to capture the "vital signs" of the job seeker's search—no matter what other questions, features, or products they were testing. By doing this, the team was able to establish a baseline and address bigger trends over time. The findings about SMS would not have changed the team's understanding of their audience if they'd represented just a few anecdotal data points. But aggregated over time, these data points became part of a very powerful dataset.

When planning your research, it's important to consider not just the urgent questions—the things you want to learn over the next few weeks. You should also consider the big questions. You still need to plan big standalone studies to get at some of these questions. But with some planning, you should be able to work a lot of long-term learning into your weekly studies.

Test What You've Got

To maintain a regular cadence of user testing, your team must adopt a "test what you got" policy. Whatever is ready on testing day is what goes in front of the users. This policy liberates your team from rushing toward testing day deadlines. Instead, you'll find yourself taking advantage of your weekly test sessions to get insight on whatever is ready, and this will create insight for you at every stage of design and development. You must, however, set expectations properly for the type of feedback you'll be able to generate with each type of artifact.

Sketches

Feedback collected on sketches helps you validate the value of your concept (Figure 6-4). They're great conversation prompts to support interviews, and they help to make abstract concepts concrete, which helps generate shared understanding. What you *won't* get from sketches is detailed, step-by-step feedback on the process, insight about specific design elements, or even meaningful feedback on copy choices. You won't be able to learn much (if anything) about the usability of your concept.

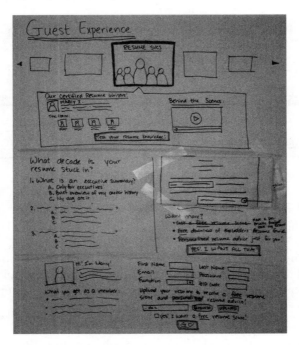

Figure 6-4. *Example of a sketch that can be used with customers*

Static wireframes

Showing test participants wireframes (Figure 6-5) lets you assess the information hierarchy and layout of your experience. In addition, you'll get feedback on taxonomy, navigation, and information architecture.

You'll receive the first trickles of workflow feedback, but at this point your test participants are focused primarily on the words on the page and the selections they're making. Wireframes provide a good opportunity to begin testing copy choices.

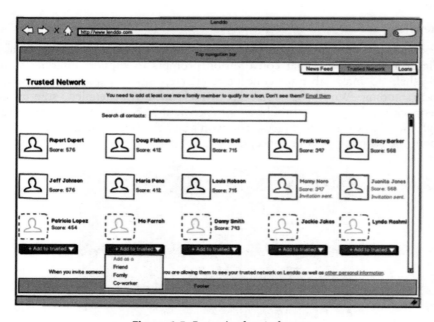

Figure 6-5. *Example of a wireframe*

High-fidelity visual mockups (not clickable)

Moving into high-fidelity visual-design assets, you receive much more detailed feedback. Test participants will be able to respond to branding, aesthetics, and visual hierarchy, as well as aspects of figure/ground relationships, grouping of elements, and the clarity of your calls to action. Your test participants will also (almost certainly) weigh in on the effectiveness of your color palette. (See Figure 6-6.)

Nonclickable mockups still don't let your customers interact naturally with the design or experience the workflow of your solution. Instead of watching your users click, tap, and swipe, you need to ask them what they would expect and then validate those responses against your planned experience.

Figure 6-6. *Example of mockup from Skype in the Classroom (design by Made By Many)*

Clickable mockups

Clickable mockups, like that shown in Figure 6-6, increase the fidelity of the interaction by linking together a set of static assets into a simulation of the product experience. Visually, they can be high, medium, or even low fidelity. The value here is not so much the visual polish, but rather the ability to simulate workflow and to observe how users interact with your designs.

Designers used to have limited tool choices for creating clickable mockups, but in recent years, we've seen a huge proliferation of tools. Some tools are optimized for making mobile mockups, others are for the web, and still others are platform-neutral. Most have no ability to work with data, but with some (like Axure), you can create basic data-driven or conditional logic-driven simulations. Additionally, design tools such as Sketch and Adobe's XD include "mirror" features with which you can see your design work in real time on mobile devices and link screens together to create prototypes without special prototyping tools.

Coded prototypes

Coded prototypes are useful because they have the best ability to deliver high fidelity in terms of *functionality*. This makes for the closest-to-real simulation that you can put in front of your users. It replicates the design, behavior, and workflow of your product. You can test with real data. You can integrate with other systems. All of this makes coded prototypes very powerful; it also makes them the most complex to produce. But because the feedback you gain is based on such a close simulation, you can treat that feedback as more authoritative than the feedback you gain from other simulations.

Monitoring Techniques for Continuous and Collaborative Discovery

In the preceding discussions, we looked at ways to use qualitative research on a regular basis to evaluate your hypotheses. However, as soon as you launch your product or feature, your customers will begin giving you constant feedback—and not only on your product. They will tell you about themselves, about the market, about the competition. This insight is invaluable—and it comes in to your organization from every corner. Seek out these treasure troves of customer intelligence within your organization and harness them to drive your ongoing product design and research, as depicted in Figure 6-7.

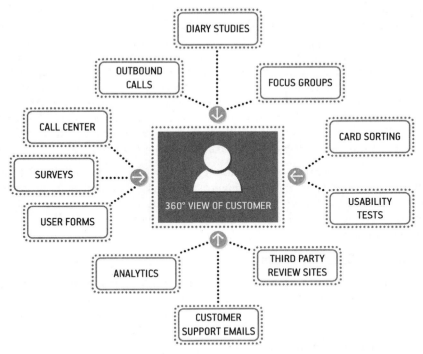

Figure 6-7. *Customers can provide feedback through many channels*

Customer Service

Customer support agents talk to more customers on a daily basis than you will talk to over the course of an entire project. There are multiple ways to harness their knowledge:

- Reach out to them and ask them what they're hearing from customers about the sections of the product on which you're working.

- Hold regular monthly meetings with them to understand the trends. What do customers love this month? What do they hate?

- Tap into their deep product knowledge to learn how they would solve the challenges your team is working on. Include them in design sessions and design reviews.

- Incorporate your hypotheses into their call scripts—one of the cheapest ways to test your ideas is to suggest it as a fix to customers calling in with a relevant complaint.

In the mid-2000s, Jeff ran the UX team at a mid-sized tech company in Portland, Oregon. One of the ways that team prioritized the work they did was by regularly checking the pulse of the customer base. The team did this with a standing monthly meeting with customer service representatives. Each month Customer Service would provide the UX team with the top 10 things customers were complaining about. The UX team then used this information to focus their efforts and to subsequently measure the efficacy of their work. At the end of the month, the next conversation with Customer Service gave the team a clear indication of whether or not their efforts were bearing fruit. If the issue was not receding in the top-10 list, the solutions had not worked.

This approach generated an additional benefit. The Customer Service team realized there was someone listening to their insights and began proactively sharing customer feedback above and beyond the monthly meeting. The dialogue that created provided the UX team with a continuous feedback loop to inform and test product hypotheses.

On-Site Feedback Surveys

Set up a feedback mechanism in your product with which customers can send you their thoughts regularly. Here are a few options:

- Simple email forms
- Customer support forums
- Third-party community sites

You can repurpose these tools for research by doing things like the following:

- Counting how many inbound emails you're getting from a particular section of the site
- Participating in online discussions and testing some of your hypotheses
- Exploring community sites to discover and recruit hard-to-find types of users

These inbound customer feedback channels provide feedback from the point of view of your most active and engaged customers. Here are a few tactics for getting other points of view.

Search logs

Search terms are clear indicators of what customers are seeking on your site. Search patterns indicate what they're finding and what they're not finding. Repeated queries with slight variations show a user's challenge in finding certain information.

One way to use search logs for MVP validation is to launch a test page for the feature you're planning. Following the search, logs will inform you as to whether the test content (or feature) on that page is meeting the user's needs. If users continue to search on variations of that content, your experiment has failed.

Site usage analytics

Site usage logs and analytics packages—especially funnel analyses—show how customers are using the site, where they're dropping off, and how they try to manipulate the product to do the things they need or expect it to do. Understanding these reports provides real-world context for the decisions the team needs to make.

In addition, use analytics tools to determine the success of experiments that have launched publicly. How has the experiment shifted usage of the product? Are your efforts achieving the outcome you defined? These tools provide an unbiased answer.

If you're just starting to build a product, *build usage analytics into it from day one*. Third-party products like Kiss Metrics and MixPanel make it easy and inexpensive to implement this functionality, and provide invaluable information to support continuous learning.

A/B testing

A/B testing is a technique, originally developed by marketers, to gauge which of two (or more) relatively similar concepts achieve the defined goal more effectively. When applied in the Lean UX framework, A/B testing becomes a powerful tool to determine the validity of your hypotheses. Applying A/B testing is relatively straightforward after your ideas evolve into working code. Here's how it works:

1. Take the proposed solution and release it to your audience. However, instead of letting every customer see it, release it only to a small subset of users.

2. Measure the performance of your solution for that audience. Compare it to the other group (your control cohort) and note the differences.

3. Did your new idea move the needle in the right direction? If it did, you've got a winning idea.

4. If not, you've got an audience of customers that might make good targets for further research. What did they think of the new experience? Would it make sense to reach out to them for some qualitative research?

The tools for A/B testing are widely available and can be inexpensive. There are third-party commercial tools like Optimizely. There also are open source A/B testing frameworks available for every major platform. Regardless of the tools you choose, the trick is to make sure the changes you're making are small enough and the population you select large enough that any change in behavior can be attributed with confidence to the change you've made. If you change too many things, any behavioral change cannot be directly attributed to your exact hypothesis.

Wrapping Up

In this chapter, we covered many ways to validate your hypotheses. We looked at collaborative discovery and continuous learning techniques. We discussed how to build a weekly Lean testing process and covered what you should test and what to expect from those tests. We looked at ways to monitor your customer experience in a Lean UX context and we touched on the power of A/B testing.

These techniques, used in conjunction with the processes outlined in Chapter 3, Chapter 4, and Chapter 5, make up the full Lean UX process loop. Your goal is to get through this loop as often as possible, refining your thinking with each iteration.

In the next section, we move away from process and take a look at how to integrate Lean UX into your organization. We'll cover the organizational shifts you'll need to make to support the Lean UX approach, whether you're a startup, large company, or a digital agency.

PART III

LEAN UX IN YOUR ORGANIZATION

Integrating design into Agile development is never easy. Sometimes, it causes a lot of pain and heartache. Jeff learned that first-hand when he was at TheLadders. After spending some time trying to integrate UX work with an Agile process, Jeff was feeling pretty good—until one morning when his UX team delivered the diagram shown in Figure III-1. This diagram visualized all of the challenges the team was facing as they tried to integrate its practice into the Agile environment. It served, initially, as a large slice of humble pie. Ultimately, though, it provided the beginning of conversations that helped Jeff, his UX team, and the rest of TheLadders' product development staff build an integrated, collaborative practice.

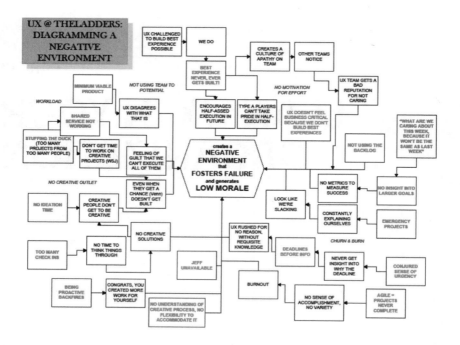

Figure III-1. *The UX team at TheLadders expressed their feelings about our Agile/UX integration efforts*

In the years since this diagram was created, we've been fortunate to work at a consulting firm that we helped found. At Neo, the work we did with companies spanned a broad range of industries, company sizes, and cultures. We helped media organizations figure out new ways to deliver and monetize their content. We built new, mobile-first sales tools for a commercial furniture manufacturer. We consulted with fashion retailers, automotive services companies, and large banks to help them build Lean UX practices. We worked with nonprofits to create new service offerings. And we trained countless teams.

Each of these projects provided us a bit more insight into how Lean UX works in that environment. We used that insight to make each subsequent project that much more successful. We've built up a body of knowledge over the past five years that has given us a clear sense of what needs to happen—at the team and at the organization level—for Lean UX to succeed. This is the focus of Part III.

Chapter 7 discusses how Lean UX fits into an Agile environment.

Chapter 8 digs into the specific organizational changes that you need to make to support this way of working. It's not just software developers and designers who need to find a way to work together: your entire product development engine is going to need to change if you want to create a truly Agile organization.

Chapter 9 presents a set of case studies that showcase how these tactics and organizational shifts have succeeded at a variety of companies.

CHAPTER 7

Integrating Lean UX and Agile

Agile methods are mainstream now. At the same time, thanks to the huge success of products like Amazon's Kindle and Apple's iPhone, so is User Experience (UX) design. But making Agile work with UX continues to be a challenge for many companies. In this chapter, we review how Lean UX methods can fit within the most popular flavor of Agile—Scrum—and discuss how blending Lean UX and Agile can create a more productive team and a more collaborative process. Here's what this chapter covers:

Definition of terms
Just to make sure we're all on the same page when we say certain words like "sprint" and "story."

Staggered sprints
The once-savior of Agile/UX integration is now just a stepping stone to true team cohesion.

Sprint zero and design sprints
How much, if any, upfront work should we do?

Dual-track Agile
How to plan product discovery activities along with delivery.

Listening to Scrum's rhythms
The meeting cadences of Scrum make for clear guide posts for Lean UX integration.

Participation
A truly cross-functional process requires that everyone be a part of it.

Design is a team sport
   Opening up the design process to all team members.

Coordinating multiple Lean UX teams
   How to encourage sharing and reduce duplicate work.

Managing up and out
   Clear obstacles to your team's progress by being proactive with your communications.

Let's get started.

Some Definitions

Agile processes like Scrum use many proprietary terms. Over time, many of these terms have taken on a life of their own. To ensure that the way we're using them is clear, we've taken the time to define a few of them here. (If you're familiar with Agile, you can skip this section.)

Scrum
   An Agile methodology promoting time-boxed cycles, team self-organization, and high team accountability. Scrum is the most popular form of Agile.

User story
   The smallest unit of work expressed as a benefit to the end user. Typical user stories are written using the following syntax:

   As a [user type]

   I want to [accomplish something]

   So that [some benefit happens]

Backlog
   A prioritized list of user stories. The backlog is the most powerful project management tool in Agile. It is through the active grooming of the backlog that the team manages their daily workload and refocuses their efforts based on incoming learnings. It is how the team stays Agile.

Sprint
   A single cycle of work for a team. The goal of each sprint is to deliver working software. Most Scrum teams work in two-week sprints.

Stand-up
   A daily, short team meeting during which each member addresses the day's challenges. This is one of Scrum's self-accountability tools. Every day,

members must declare to their teammates what they're doing and what's getting in their way.

Retrospective

A meeting at the end of each sprint that takes an honest look at what went well, what went poorly, and how the team will try to improve process in the next sprint. Your process is as iterative as your product. Retrospectives give your team the chance to optimize your process with every sprint.

Iteration planning meeting

A meeting at the beginning of each sprint during which the team plans what they'll be doing during the upcoming sprint. Sometimes, this meeting includes estimation and story gathering. This is the meeting that determines the initial prioritization of the backlog.

Product discovery

A term used to describe any learning activities the team undertakes to help them determine what to deliver. Lean UX powers the product discovery process.

Sprint zero

This is the time before product delivery begins that many organizations set aside for product discovery. It can extend beyond one sprint. Our goal is to ensure that, even if you're using the sprint-zero model, it is not the only time that testing, learning, and validation take place.

Design sprint

A term popularized by the design team at Google Ventures used to describe a time-boxed collection of collaborative activities that help a team move quickly from ideas to prototypes. Running a design sprint as "sprint zero" is an increasingly common practice.

Dual-track Agile

Popularized by product management guru Marty Cagan, dual-track Agile is an attempt to build a continuous product discovery and delivery model for Scrum teams. It champions a process in which teams manage two backlogs—a discovery backlog and a delivery backlog. They work through their discovery backlogs with only validated items graduating into the delivery cycle. In many ways, if executed well, this is the end state most teams should strive for; however, it is not without its challenges.

Staggered Sprints and Their Modern Offshoots

In May 2007, Desiree Sy and Lynn Miller published "Adapting Usability Investigations for Agile User-centered Design" in the *Journal of Usability Studies*.[1] Sy and Miller were some of the first people to try to combine Agile and UX, and many of us were excited by the solutions they were proposing. In the 2007 article, Sy and Miller describe in detail their idea of a productive integration of Agile and User-Centered Design. They called it *cycle 0* (though it has come to be referred to popularly as either "sprint zero" or sometimes "staggered sprints").

In short, Sy and Miller described a process in which design activity takes place one sprint ahead of development. Work is designed and validated during the "design sprint" and then passed off into the development stream to be implemented during the development sprint, as is illustrated in Figure 7-1.

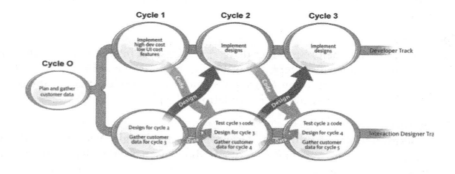

Figure 7-1. *Sy and Miller's "Staggered Sprints" model*

Many teams have misinterpreted this model, though. Sy and Miller always advocated strong collaboration between designers and developers during *both* the design *and* development sprints. Many teams have missed this critical point and instead have created workflows in which designers and developers communicate by handoff—creating a kind of mini-waterfall process.

Staggered sprints can work well for some teams. If your development environment does not allow for frequent releases (for example, you work on embedded software, or deliver software to an environment in which continuous

---

1 Desirée Sy, "Adapting Usability Investigations for Agile User-centered Design", *Journal of Usability Studies*, May 2007 (http://www.upassoc.org/upa_publications/jus/2007may/agile-ucd.pdf).

deployment is difficult or impossible),[2] the premium on getting the design right is higher. (In these cases, Lean UX might not be a great fit for your team because you'll need to work hard to get the market feedback you need to make many of these techniques work.) For these teams, staggered sprints can allow for more validation of design work—provided you are still working in a very collaborative manner. And teams transitioning from waterfall to Agile can benefit from working this way, as well, because it teaches you to work in shorter cycles, and to divide your work into sequential pieces. However, this model works best as a transition. It is not where you want your team to end up.

Here's why: it becomes very easy to create a situation in which the entire team is never working on the same thing at the same time. You never realize the benefits of cross-functional collaboration because the different disciplines are focused on different things. Without that collaboration, you don't build shared understanding, so you end up relying heavily on documentation and handoffs for communication.

There's another reason this process is less than ideal: it can create unnecessary waste. You waste time creating documentation to describe what happened during the design sprints. And, if developers haven't participated in the design sprint, they haven't had a chance to assess the work for feasibility or scope. That conversation doesn't happen until handoff. Can they actually build the specified designs in the next two weeks? If not, the work that went into designing those elements is wasted.

Evolving the Design Sprint

These days, the term "design sprint" has taken on a new meaning. The term is now associated with the ideas in the book *Sprint* by Jake Knapp, John Zeratsky, and Braden Kowitz (Simon & Schuster). They describe a design sprint as a way to bring together all the key stakeholders on a new project or initiative. Working closely together over the course of five days, this cross-functional team brainstorms, iterates, and works their way through a series of ideas. The week culminates with a prototype. In most cases, the resulting prototype has even had a round or two of customer research applied to it.

This is a technique that we've used many times in our own practice (based on the time-honored Design Studio method, described in Chapter 4). It is highly effective at bringing together a diverse set of colleagues, exposing their

---

2 Teams that work on mobile apps fall into a gray zone here. You can update frequently, but not continuously, so you'll need to become crafty with your techniques. Using feature flags to turn some features on and off can help. You can also deliver experimental features inside apps by using a browser container within the app itself. Finally, it's possible to test really early versions of features on the mobile web.

assumptions and biases about the business problem at hand and injecting these opinions with a dose of market reality. In our experience, the ideal result of a design sprint is a backlog of hypotheses. This prioritized list of risks defines the work that the team must continue to validate throughout the project lifecycle. Design sprints also help us to better define the scope of our work—at least for the foreseeable future—allowing teams, both in-house and consulting, to provide their stakeholders with a more accurate timeline for product launch.

There are a few pitfalls to watch out for when running a full five-day design sprint:

Use them on the right projects
Ensure that the problem space you're exploring is big enough to warrant putting your entire team in a room for five days. New projects, initiatives, or business lines are worthy of this process. Smaller changes to existing workflows might be too small to warrant a full design sprint.

Keep the team size small
Design sprints are touted as a great tool for collaboration. This is true, but collaboration can get diluted if too many people are involved. Run these sprints with the core team and their immediate stakeholders. Try to keep the participant number to about 10 people.

Adapt the recipe to your needs
There are many detailed descriptions of exactly how to facilitate a design sprint. These are phenomenal resources for early practitioners of this technique. But don't become stuck following the rules. As you gain experience with design sprints, ask yourself which elements of the design sprint add value given your current project and time constraints, and which can be discarded to save time.

Learning doesn't end at the end of the design sprint
Design sprints are exciting, high-energy bursts of work. But it's hard to sustain that energy. We've seen teams emerge energized and motivated to get building. But learning shouldn't end when the design sprint ends. As the product progresses and evolves, new questions will come up, and they require further discovery. Ensure that elements of the design sprint make their way into future sprints so that your team doesn't end up implementing blindly.

Dual-Track Agile

In many ways, dual-track Agile is what Sy and Miller were trying to convey with their staggered-sprint model. Marty Cagan, Jeff Patton, and others advocate for a process in which a single team manages two backlogs: a discovery backlog and a delivery backlog. The team splits into two units to do the work: a discovery unit and a delivery unit. The discovery unit works through the discovery items, running experiments and speaking to customers in an effort to discover which ideas merit further exploration and which don't. Ideas that graduate from discovery to delivery are built by the delivery unit of the team. This reduces the amount of documentation necessary to drive the delivery process because the people who validated the feature are in close contact with, or in some cases are, the same people who design and implement it. Figure 7-2 offers an overview of the process.

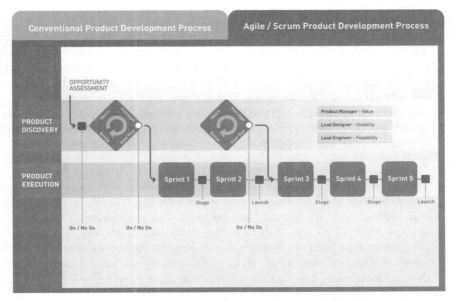

Figure 7-2. *Marty Cagan's dual-track Agile process diagram (image courtesy of Marty Cagan)*

Theoretically, dual-track Agile promises to manage learning and delivery in a transparent way. It allows the team to prioritize their work based on evidence while using that same evidence to provide their stakeholders with regular updates, directional shifts, and data. In practice though, we've seen teams hit the following speed bumps:

Separate discovery and delivery teams

One antipattern we've witnessed several times is teams splitting up who does the discovery and who does the delivery on their team. Often the UX designer and/or the product manager take on the bulk of the discovery work. The engineers are delegated early delivery work. This effectively recreates the mini-waterfalls of staggered sprints, as described earlier. The shared understanding breaks down, slowing the pace of decision-making and reducing the team's cohesion, productivity, and learning. Our recommendation is to have as many team members involved in discovery as possible, especially early on in an initiative, so that the core decisions about your project are made with everyone's participation. As the project continues, there will certainly be situations in which not everyone is available for research work. In these cases, those who do the research are responsible for bringing it back to the team as soon as it's over and discussing their findings while they're fresh.

Limited knowledge of how to do discovery

Building a dual-track Agile process assumes that your team knows how to do discovery. There are many tools that you can use to build feedback loops into a discovery backlog. Without a broader knowledge of these tools, teams resort to the ones they're most familiar with, and often pick suboptimal tactics for learning. If you have access to researchers, try to add them to your team. At the very least, seek out their input as new discovery initiatives begin. Seasoned practitioners can teach your team the best method for your needs and can help you plan your discovery work.

Not feeding back evidence from the delivery work to the discovery backlog

This challenge is symptomatic of an organization that is still thinking incrementally. After a feature makes it from discovery to delivery, the team will implement it as designed and ship it. The great thing about that is that, as soon as it's live, this new feature begins to provide a new set of data about how well it's working and where to focus your next discovery activities. Ensure that your team is continuing to collect feedback on shipped features and using that information to regularly assess the prioritization of their discovery work.

Exploiting the Rhythms of Scrum to Build a Lean UX Practice

Over the years, we've found some useful ways to integrate Lean UX approaches with the rhythms of Scrum. Let's take a look at how you can use Scrum's meeting cadence and Lean UX to build an efficient process.

Themes

Scrum has a lot of meetings. Many people frown on meetings, but if you use them as mileposts during your sprint you can create an integrated Lean UX and Agile process in which the entire team is working on the same thing at the same time.

Let's assume that you've chosen a risky hypothesis as the early focus of your project. You can use that hypothesis to create a theme that guides the work you'll do over the next set of sprints, as demonstrated in Figure 7-3.

Figure 7-3. *Sprints tied together with a theme*

Kick Off the Theme with a Design Sprint

Start work on each theme with some version of a Design Studio or design sprint. (See Figure 7-4.) Depending on the scope of the hypothesis, the design sprint can be as short as an afternoon or as long as a week. You can do them with your immediate team but should include a broader group if it's a larger-scale effort. (See Chapter 4 for details on how to run a Design Studio.) The point of this kickoff is to get the entire team sketching, ideating, and speaking to customers together, creating a backlog of ideas from which to test and learn. In addition, this activity will help define the scope of your theme a bit better—assuming that you've built in some customer feedback loops.

After you've started your regular sprints, your ideas will be tested, validated, and developed: new insights will come in, and you'll need to decide what to do with them. You make these decisions by running subsequent shorter brainstorming sessions and collaborative discovery activities before each new sprint begins. This allows the team to use the latest insight to create the backlog for the next sprint.

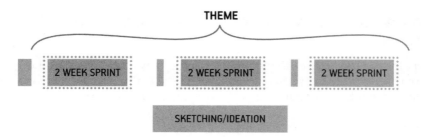

Figure 7-4. *Timing and scope of design sprints*

Iteration Planning Meeting

Bring the output of your design sprint to the iteration planning meeting (IPM). Your mess of sticky notes, sketches, wireframes, paper prototypes, and any other artifacts might seem useless to outside observers but will be meaningful to your team. You made these artifacts together and because of that you have the shared understanding necessary to extract stories from them. Use them in your IPM to write user stories together, and then estimate and prioritize the stories. (See Figure 7-5.)

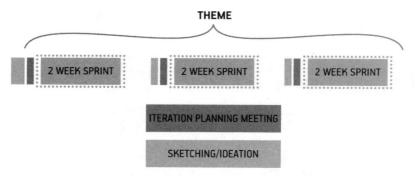

Figure 7-5. *Hold iteration planning meetings immediately after brainstorming sessions*

Experiment Stories

As you plan your iteration, there might be additional discovery work that needs to be done during the iteration that wasn't covered in the design sprint or collaborative discovery activities. Or, there might be work in your discovery backlog that you know is coming up that needs to happen by a certain time frame. To accommodate this in your sprint cadence use experiment stories. Captured by using the same method as your user stories, experiment stories have two distinct benefits:

They visualize discovery work
> Discovery work is not inherently tangible as delivery work can be. Experiment stories solve that by leveling the playing field. Everything your team works on—discovery or delivery—goes on the backlog as a story.

They force its prioritization against delivery work
> After those stories are in the backlog, you need to put them in priority order. This forces conversations around *when* to run the experiment and, equally as important, what we *won't* be working on during that same time.

Experiment stories look just like user stories, as illustrated in Figure 7-6.

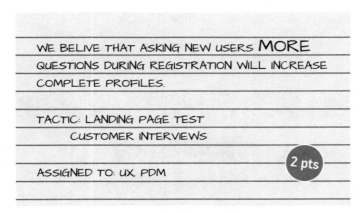

Figure 7-6. *Experiment stories*

Experiment stories contain the following elements:

- The hypothesis you're testing or the thing you're trying to learn
- Tactic(s) for learning (e.g., customer interviews, A/B tests, and prototypes)
- Who will do the work
- A level of effort estimate (if you do estimations) for how much work you expect this to be

After they are written, experiment stories go into your backlog. When their time comes up in the sprint, that's the assigned person's main focus. When the experiment is over, bring the findings to the team immediately and discuss them to determine the impact of these findings. Your team should be ready to change course, even within the current sprint, if the outcome of the experiment stories reveals insights that invalidate your current prioritization.

User Validation Schedule

Finally, to ensure that you have a constant stream of customer feedback to use for your experiments, plan user research sessions every single week. (See Figure 7-7.) This way your team is never more than five business days away from customer feedback and has ample time to react prior to the end of the sprint. This weekly research cadence provides a good rhythm for your experiment stories as well as a natural learning point in the sprint.

Use the artifacts you created in the ideation sessions as the base material for your user tests. Remember that when the ideas are raw, you are testing for value (that is, *do people want to use my product?*). After you have established that there is a desire for your product, subsequent tests with higher-fidelity artifacts will reveal whether your solution is usable.

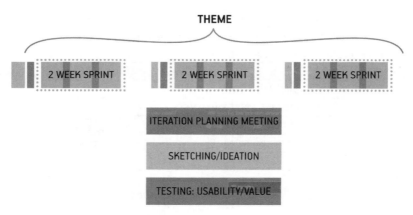

Figure 7-7. *Conversations with users happen every week*

Participation

Agile methods can create a lot of time pressure on designers. Some work fits easily into the context of a user story. Other work needs more time to get right. Two-week cycles of concurrent development and design offer few opportunities for designers to ruminate on big problems. And although some Agile methods take a more flexible approach to time than Scrum does (for example, Kanban does away with the notion of a two-week batch of work, and places the emphasis on continuous flow), most designers feel pressure to fit their work into the time-box of the sprint. For this reason, designers need to participate in the sprint-planning process.

The major reason designers feel pressure in Agile processes is that they don't (for whatever reason) fully participate in the process. This is typically not their fault: when Agile is understood as simply a way to build software, there doesn't appear to be any reason to include nontechnologists in the process. However, without designer participation, their concerns and needs are not taken into account in project plans. As a result, many Agile teams don't make plans that allow designers to do their best work.

For Lean UX to work in Agile, the entire team must participate in all activities —stand-ups, retrospectives, IPMs, brainstorming sessions—they all require everyone's attendance to be successful. Besides negotiating the complexity of certain features, cross-functional participation allows designers and developers to create effective backlog prioritization.

For example, imagine at the beginning of a sprint that the first story a team prioritizes has a heavy design component to it. Imagine that the designer was not there to voice her concern. That team will fail as soon as they meet for their stand-up the next day. The designer will cry out that the story has not been designed. She will say that it will take at least two to three days to complete the design before the story is ready for development. Imagine instead that the designer had participated in the prioritization of the backlog. Her concern would have been raised at planning time. The team could have selected a story card that needed less design preparation to work on first—which would have bought the designer the time she needed to complete the work.

The other casualty of sparse participation is shared understanding. Teams make decisions in meetings. Those decisions are based on discussions. Even if 90 percent of a meeting is not relevant to your immediate need, the 10 percent that is relevant will save hours of time downstream explaining what happened at the meeting and why certain decisions were made.

Participation gives you the ability to negotiate for the time you need to do your work. This is true for UX designers as much as it is for everyone else on the team.

Design Is a Team Sport

In the following case study, designer and coach Lane Goldstone details how she brought to the table all the players—development, design, marketing, stakeholders—to create a tablet game.

Case Study: *Knowsy* (by Lane Goldstone)

In my work as a product designer, I use Lean UX practices on a variety of projects. Recently I've worked on entertainment, ecommerce, and social-media products for different platforms, including iPad, iPhone, and the Web. The teams have been small, ranging from three to seven people. Most of my projects also share the following characteristics:

- The project is run within an Agile framework (focus on the customer, continuous delivery, team sits together, lightweight documentation, team ownership of decisions, shared rituals like stand-ups, retrospectives, and so on).
- The team contains people with a mix of skills (frontend and backend development, user experience and information architecture, product management and marketing, graphic design, and copywriting).
- The people on the team generally performed in their area of expertise/strength, but were supportive of other specialties and interested in learning new skills.

Most of the teams I work with create entirely new products or services. They are not working within an existing product framework or structure. In "green fields" projects like these, we are simultaneously trying to discover how this new product or service will be used, how it will behave, and how we are going to build it. It's an environment of continual change, and there isn't a lot of time or patience for planning or up-front design.

The Innovation Games Company

The Innovation Games Company (TIGC) produces serious games—online and in-person—for market research. TIGC helps organizations get actionable insights into customer needs and preferences to improve performance through collaborative play. In 2010, I was invited to help TIGC create a new game for the consumer market.

I was part of the team that created *Knowsy* for iPad (Figure 7-8), a pass-'n'-play game that's all about learning what you know about your friends, family, and coworkers—while simultaneously testing how well they know you. The person who knows the other players best wins the game. It is fast, fun, and a truly "social" game for up to six players.

It was our first iPad application, and we had an ambitious deadline: one month to create the game and have it accepted to the Apple Store. Our small team had a combination of subject-matter expertise and skills in frontend and backend development as well as visual and interaction design. We also drew on the help of other people to help us play-test the game at various stages of development.

Figure 7-8. *The Knowsy team with the wall of artifacts behind them*

A Shared Vision Empowers Independent Work

Until a new product is coded, it's difficult for people to work within the same product vision. *You can recognize a lack of shared vision when the team argues about what features are important or what should be done first.* There can also be a general sense of tension that the team is not "moving fast enough" or it feels like the team is going back over the same issues again and again.

While working on *Knowsy*, I looked for ways that I could make my UX practice more quick, visual, collaborative, and continuous. I looked for opportunities to work in real time with other people on the team (such as developers and the product manager) and rough things out as quickly as possible at the lowest responsible level of fidelity.

As we found the appropriate solutions and the team understood and bought into the design concept, I was able to increase fidelity of the design artifacts, confident that we shared a product vision.

Breaking the Design Bottleneck

Early in the project, I sat with the frontend developer to talk about the game design. We created a high-level game flow together on paper (Figure 7-9), passing the marker back and forth as we talked. This was my opportunity to listen and learn what he was thinking. As we sketched, I was able to point out inconsistencies by asking questions like, "What do we do when *this* happens?" This approach had the benefit of changing the dialog from, "I'm right-you're wrong," to "How do we solve this problem?"

After we had this basic agreement, I was able to create a paper prototype of the game based on the flow and we play tested it with the team. The effect on the team was immediate. Suddenly, everyone "got it" and was excited about what we were doing. People began to contribute ideas that fit well together, and we were able to identify what parts we could each work on that supported the whole.

When we were all on the same page, it was easier for me to take some time away from the team and document what we'd agreed in a clickable prototype.

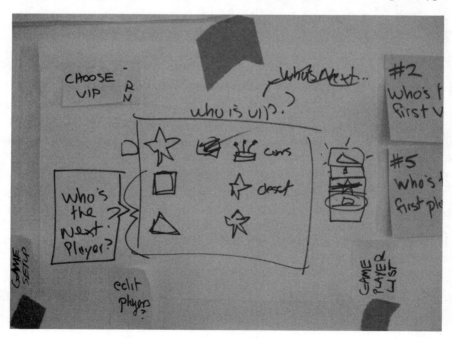

Figure 7-9. *The paper prototype begins to take shape*

The Outcome

Knowsy's foray into Lean UX proved a success. We got the app to the Apple Store in time for the deadline. I was called back later to help the team do another variant of the product. For that go-around, I used a similar process. Because I was working remotely and the development team was not as available to collaborate, I had to make heavier deliverables. Nevertheless, the basic principle of iterating our way to higher fidelity continued.

Figure 7-10. *Lane updating the prototype and artifact wall in real time*

Beyond the Scrum Team

Management check-ins are one of the biggest obstacles to maintaining team momentum. Designers are used to doing design reviews, but unfortunately, check-ins don't end there. Product owners, stakeholders, CEOs, and clients all want to know how things are going. They all want to bless the project plan going forward. The challenge for outcome-focused teams is that their project plans are dependent on what they are learning. They are responsive, so their typical plan lays out only small batches of work at a time. At most, these teams plan an iteration or two ahead. This perceived "short-sightedness" tends not to satisfy most high-level managers. How then do you keep the check-ins at bay while maintaining the pace of your Lean UX and Scrum processes?

Two words: *proactive communication.*

Jeff once managed a team that radically altered the workflow for an existing product that had thousands of paying customers. The team was so excited by the changes they'd made that they went ahead with the launch without alerting anyone else in the organization. Within an hour of the new product going live the vice president of customer service was at Jeff's desk, fuming and demanding to know why she wasn't told of this change. The issue was this: when customers have problems with the product, they call in for help. Call center representatives use scripts to troubleshoot customer problems and to offer solutions —except they didn't have a script for this new product. Because they didn't know it was going to change.

This healthy slice of humble pie served as a valuable lesson. If you want your stakeholders—both those managing you and those dependent on you—to stay out of your way, make sure that they are aware of your plans. Here are a few tips:

- Maintain a "Problem Roadmap." Instead of using a feature roadmap to communicate with stakeholders, transform the roadmap to communicate the *problems* you'll be working on. Use this Problem Roadmap to drive planning and check-in meetings with stakeholders.
- Proactively reach out to your product owners and executives to keep them updated on your plans.
- Let them know:
  — how the project is going;
  — what you tried so far and learned;
  — what you'll be trying next;
  — what risks you see in the product and how you plan to address them.
- Keep the conversations focused on outcomes (how you're trending toward your goal) not feature sets.
- Ensure dependent departments (customer service, marketing, operations, etc.) are aware of upcoming changes that can affect their world.
- Provide them with plenty of time to update their workflows if necessary.

Lean UX and Agile in the Enterprise

Many of the tactics covered in this book are focused on one team. But in the real world, enterprise organizations have multiple product development teams working in parallel. How does Lean UX scale when the number of teams grows to tens or even hundreds of concurrent workstreams? This is the question of the moment in the Agile community. As Lean and Agile methods have become more mainstream, and as they have become the default working style for technology teams across industries, many people have become focused on this question. Large organizations have a legitimate need to coordinate the activity of multiple teams—processes based on *learning your way forward* present a challenge to most traditional project management methods.

A full discussion of how to create a truly Agile and Lean organization is beyond the scope of this book. It requires leadership to radically rethink the way it sets strategy, assembles teams, and plans and assigns work. That said, there are a few techniques that can help Lean UX scale in enterprise Agile environments and even take advantage of that scale. Here are just a few issues that typically arise and ways to manage for them:

Issue

As projects grow bigger, more teams are assigned to them. How do you ensure that all teams are aligned to the same vision and not optimizing locally?

Solution

The concept of managing to outcomes applies to a set of teams as much as it does to individual ones. To ensure that all the teams working on the same project have a shared vision, assign them all the same success metric. Working together, they can define the leading indicators that drive that metric and divide those leading metrics between the teams on the project. But teams must not be allowed to focus on leading metrics to the exclusion of the larger outcome: the entire set of teams succeeds only if they hit the overarching outcome together.

Issue

How do you ensure that teams are sharing what they're learning and minimizing duplicate effort to learn the same things?

Solution

Although there's no silver bullet to solve for this issue, the successful practices we've seen include a central knowledge management tool (like a wiki), regular team leadership meetings (like a Scrum of Scrums), and open-communication tools that focus on research (like a dedicated channel on Slack or your internal chat tool).

Issue

Cross-team dependencies can keep progress at a crawl. How do you maintain a regular pace of learning and delivery in a multiteam environment?

Solution

Create self-sufficient "full-stack" teams. Full-stack teams have every capability needed for them to do their work on the team. This doesn't mean that they need a person from each department—just that there is someone on the team who can do one or more of the things the team might need. The specific disciplines on the team—designers, content people, frontend developers, backend developers, product managers—coordinate with one another at discipline-specific meetings to ensure that they are up-to-date on their practice, but the work takes place locally.

Wrapping Up

This chapter took a closer look at how Lean UX fits into an Agile process. In addition, we looked at how cross-functional collaboration allows a team to move forward at a brisk pace, and how to handle stakeholders and managers who always want to know what's going on. We discussed why having everyone participate in all activities is critical and how the staggered-sprint model, once considered the path to true agility, has evolved into design sprints and dual-track product discovery and delivery.

In the next chapter, we take a look at the organizational shifts that need to be made to support Lean UX. This chapter can serve as a primer for managers on what they'll need to do to set teams up for success.

CHAPTER 8

Making Organizational Shifts

In baseball, you don't know nothing.
—**Yogi Berra**

In Part I of this book, we discussed the principles behind Lean UX. We hope you understand from that section that Lean UX is a mindset. In Part II, we discussed some of the key methods of Lean UX, because Lean UX is also a process. As we've worked with clients and taught these methods to teams, it's become clear that Lean UX is also a management method. For this reason, you'll need to make some changes in your organization to get the most benefit from working this way.

Organizational shifts aren't easy, but they're not optional. The world has changed: our organizations must change with it. Any business of scale (or any business that seeks to scale) is, like it or not, in the software business. Regardless of the industry in which your company operates, software has become central to delivering your product or service.

This is both empowering and threatening. The ability to reach global markets, scale operations to meet increased demand, and create a continuous conversation with your customers has never been easier. This power is also a double-edged sword: it offers these same opportunities to smaller competitors who would never have been able to compete before the broad adoption of software. This makes the need to adopt Lean UX all the more urgent.

Lean UX makes it possible for you to use the power of software to create a continuous improvement loop that allows your company to stay ahead of its competitors. It's this loop that drives organizational agility and allows your company to react to changes in the market at speeds never possible, even just five years ago.

The Shifts

When we train teams, they sometimes ask, "How can we put these methods into practice here?" And on this point, we're always a little hesitant. Although we're confident that most organizations can solve these problems, we're also aware that every organization is different. Finding the right solution requires a lot of close work and collaboration with your colleagues and your executives.

To prepare you for that work, we're going to use this chapter to share some of the shifts that organizations need to make in order to embrace Lean UX. We're not going to tell you *how* to make those shifts; that's your job. But we hope this discussion will help you survey the landscape to find the areas you're going to want to address.

In this chapter, we discuss the shifts your organization might need to make in these areas.

Changing Culture

As you implement Lean UX, consider these dimensions of culture:

- Adopting a position of humility
- Embracing new skills
- Creating open, collaborative workspaces
- No more heroes
- Falling in love with the problem, not the solution
- Shifting agency culture
- Being realistic about your environment

Shifting Team Organization

To implement Lean UX, you'll also need to rethink the way you organize teams:

- Moving from limited roles to collaborative capabilities
- Creating cross-functional teams
- Creating small teams

- Working with distributed teams
- Working with third-party vendors

Shifting Process

Finally, your product development processes will change as well:

- Shifting from output to outcomes
- Eliminating Big Design up front
- Speed first, aesthetics second
- Embracing UX debt
- Navigating documentation standards
- Managing up and out

SHIFT: Humility

Imagine for a moment that you work on an assembly line that makes cars. The end state of your product is well-defined in advance. The cost of producing that product is clear. The process to create it has been optimized and the ways customers will use that car—based on more than 100 years of observation—is also clear. In situations like this, the focus is on quality, efficiency, and cost control.

We're not building cars.

Our medium is software, and our products and services are complex and unpredictable. They don't have an end state. We can continue to design, build, operate, and optimize our digital products as long as it makes economic sense to do so. Most perplexing is that our customers might use our digital services in ways we never imagined. In many cases, the best features of a system emerge over time as people use the system. (Twitter's hashtag is a great example of this: users invented this feature, and then Twitter added support for it after the fact.) With so many unknowns, there is only so much confidence we can have in the scope, roadmap, implementation, and success of our product. The good news is that through the rise of the Agile and DevOps movements, we can move away from the assembly-line methods of past generations and adopt continuous production methods. When we pair that capability with Lean UX, we get the ability to learn very quickly how valid or invalid our ideas are.

To fully take advantage of these new capabilities, your organization must adopt a position of humility. Your organization must accept that, in the face of all this complexity and uncertainty, we just can't predict the exact shape our service will have to take to be successful. This is not an abdication of vision.

Instead, it requires a strong opinion about the shape the system *should* take, coupled with the willingness to change course if evidence from the market reveals that initial vision was wrong. Adopting this mindset makes it safe for teams to experiment, fail, and learn. It is only through this trial-and-error process that Lean UX can thrive. If there's no room for course correction, the continuous learning that Lean UX promotes will be seen, at best, as a distraction, and, at worst, a waste of time.

SHIFT: Outcomes

Chapter 3 discusses the role of *outcomes* in Lean UX. Lean UX teams measure their success not in terms of completed features, but in terms of progress toward specific outcomes. Determining outcomes is a leadership activity; it's one that many organizations are not good at or don't do at all. Too often, leadership directs the product team through a feature-centric Product Roadmap—a set of outputs and features that they require the product team to produce by a specific date.

Teams using Lean UX must be empowered to decide for themselves which features will create the outcomes their organizations require. To do this, teams must shift their conversation with leadership from one based on features to one centered on outcomes. This conversational shift is a radical one. Product managers must determine which business metrics require the most attention. What effect are they trying to create? Are they trying to influence customer behavior? If so, how? Are they trying to increase performance? If so, by what measure? These metrics must be linked to a larger business impact.

Leadership must set this direction. If not, teams must demand this shift of them. Teams must ask, *"why are we working on this project?"* And, *"how will we know we've done a good job?"* Managers need to be retrained to give their teams the answers to these questions. They must be given the freedom to work with their teams to determine which features best achieve these goals. Teams must move from feature roadmaps to backlogs of hypotheses to test. Work should be prioritized based on risk, feasibility, and potential success.

SHIFT: Roles

In most companies, the work you do is determined by your job title. That job title comes with a job description. Too often, people in organizations discourage others from working outside the confines of their job descriptions (e.g., "You're not a developer, what can you possibly know about JavaScript?") This approach is deeply anticollaborative and leaves people's full set of skills, talents, and competencies unused.

Discouraging cross-functional input encourages organizational silos. The more discrete a person's job is, the easier it becomes to retreat to the safe confines of that discipline. As a result, conversation across disciplines wanes, and mistrust, finger-pointing, and CYA ("Cover Your Ass") behavior grows.

Silos are the death of collaborative teams.

For Lean UX to succeed, your organization needs to adopt a mantra of "competencies over roles." Every team member possesses a core competency—design, software development, research, and so on—and must deliver on that skill set. However, members might also possess secondary competencies that make the team work more efficiently.

Allow your colleagues to contribute in any disciplines in which they have expertise and interest. You'll find it creates a more engaged team that can complete tasks more efficiently. You'll also find it builds camaraderie across job titles as people with different disciplines show interest in what their colleagues are doing. Teams that enjoy working together produce better work.

SHIFT: New skills for UX designers

Many companies only ask designers to create wireframes, specifications, and site maps. They limit their participation in a project to the design phase of whatever process the company happens to be using. Plugging designers into these existing workflows limits their effectiveness by limiting the scope of their work, which has a side-effect of reinforcing a siloed team model.

The success of a collaborative team demands more. Although teams still need core UX skills, designers must add facilitation as one of their core competencies. This requires two significant shifts to the way we've worked to date:

Designers must open up the design process
The team—not the individual—needs to own the product design. Instead of hiding behind a monitor for days at a time, designers need to bring their teams into the design process, seek their input, and build that insight into the design. Doing so will begin to break down silos and promote a more cross-functional conversation to take place. To do this, designers must employ a broad range of collaborative tactics, and must be both creative and deeply practical—seeking tactics that meet the team's needs, advance the conversation, and respect the realities of team capacity and project timeline.

Designers must take a leadership role on their team
Your colleagues are used to giving you critique on your design work. What they're not used to doing is co-creating that design with you. Design leadership and facilitation in group brainstorming activities like Design Studio can create safe forums for the entire team to conceptualize your product and showcase the synthesizing capabilities of the design team.

SHIFT: Cross-functional teams

For many teams, collaboration is a single-discipline activity. Developers solve problems with other developers while designers go sit on bean bags, fire up the lava lamps, and "ideate" with their black-turtlenecked brethren. (We kid.) (Well... only a little. We love designers.)

The ideas born of single-discipline collaborations are single-faceted. They don't reflect the broader perspective of the team, which can illuminate a wider range of needs, be they the needs of the customer, the business, or the technology. Worse, working this way requires discipline-based teams to explain their work. Too often, the result is a heavy reliance on detailed documentation and a slowdown in the broader team's learning pace.

Lean UX requires cross-functional collaboration. By creating interaction between product managers, developers, QA engineers, designers, and marketers, you put everyone on the same page. Equally important: you put everyone on the same level. No single discipline dictates to the other. All are working toward a common goal. Allow your designers to attend "developer meetings," and vice versa. In fact, just have team meetings.

We've known how important cross-functional collaboration is for a long time. Robert Dailey's study from the late '70s called "The Role of Team and Task Characteristics in R&D Team Collaborative Problem Solving and Productivity," found a link between a team's problem-solving productivity and what he called "four predictors," which included "task certainty, task interdependence, team size, and *team cohesiveness.*"[1]

Keep your team cohesive by breaking down the discipline-based boundaries.

SHIFT: Small teams

Larger groups of people are less efficient than smaller ones. This makes intuitive sense. But less obvious is this: a smaller team must work on smaller problems. This small size makes it easier to maintain the discipline needed to produce Minimum Viable Products (MVPs). Break your big teams into what Amazon.com founder Jeff Bezos famously called "two-pizza teams." If the team needs more than two pizzas to make a meal, it's too big.

If the task is large, break it down into components that several small teams can handle simultaneously. Align those teams with a single outcome to achieve. This way, all of them are working toward the same goal. This forces these

---

[1] Robert C. Daley, "The Role of Team and Task Characteristics in R&D Team Collaborative Problem Solving and Productivity", *Management Science*, November 1, 1978 (http://dx.doi.org/10.1287/mnsc.24.15.1579)

small teams to self-organize and communicate efficiently while reducing the risk of each team optimizing locally.

SHIFT: Workspace

Break down the physical barriers that prevent collaboration. Colocate your teams and create workspaces for them that keep everyone visible and accessible. Make space for your team to put their work up on walls and other work surfaces. Nothing is more effective than walking over to a colleague, showing some work, discussing, sketching, exchanging ideas, understanding facial expressions and body language, and reaching a resolution on a thorny topic.

When you colocate people, create cross-functional groupings. That means removing them from the comforts of their discipline's "hideout." It's amazing how even one cubicle wall can hinder conversation between colleagues.

Open workspaces make it possible for team members to see each other and to easily reach out when questions arise. Some teams have gone as far as putting their desks on wheels so that they can relocate closer to the team members they're collaborating with on that particular day. Augment these open spaces with breakout rooms where the teams can brainstorm. Wall-sized whiteboards or simply painting the walls with whiteboard paint provides many square feet of discussion space. In short, remove the physical obstacles between your team members. Your space planners might not like it at first, but your stakeholders will thank you.

SHIFT: Distributed teams

In many situations collocation is not an option. When dealing with distributed teams, give them the tools they need to communicate and collaborate. These include things like video conferencing software (e.g., Skype and Google Hangouts), real-time communication services (e.g., Slack and Hipchat), simple file-sharing software (e.g., Dropbox), remote-pairing software (Screenhero), and anything else that might make their collaboration easier and more productive. Don't forget that occasionally plane tickets to meet each other in the flesh go a long way toward maintaining long-distance collaboration. Perhaps the most important thing to remember if you're trying to implement Lean UX with distributed teams is this: the members of these teams must be awake at the same time. The overlap doesn't need to cover an entire work day but there must be some block of time every day during which colleagues can have conversations and participate in collaborative exercises.

SHIFT: No more heroes

As we've continued to work with a wider variety of teams there are still many designers who resist Lean UX. One reason? Many designers want to be heroes.

In an environment in which designers create beautiful deliverables, they can maintain a heroic aura. Requirements go in one end of the design machine and gorgeous artwork makes its way out. People "ooh" and "aah" when the design is unveiled. Designers have thrived on these reactions (both informal and formalized as awards) for many years.

We're not suggesting that all of these designs are superficial. Schooling, formal training, experience, and a healthy dose of inspiration go into every Photoshop document that designers create—and often the results are smart, well considered, and valuable. However, those glossy deliverables can drive bad corporate decisions—they can bias judgment specifically because their beauty is so persuasive. Awards are based on the aesthetics of the designs (rather than the outcome of the work), hiring decisions are made on the sharpness of wireframes, and compensation depends on the brand names attached to each of the portfolio pieces.

The result of this is that the creators of these documents are heralded as thought leaders and elevated to the top of the experience design field. They are recognized as the "go-to" people when the problem has to get solved quickly. But can a single design hero be responsible for the success of the user experience, the business, and the team? Should one person be heralded as the sole reason for an initiative's success?

In short, no.

For Lean UX to succeed in your organization, all types of contributors—designers and nondesigners—need to collaborate broadly. This can be a hard shift for some, especially for visual designers with a background in interactive agencies. In those contexts, the creative director is untouchable. In Lean UX, the only thing that's untouchable is customer insight.

Lean UX literally has no time for heroes. The entire concept of design as hypothesis immediately dethrones notions of heroism; as a designer you must expect that many of your ideas will fail in testing. Heroes don't admit failure. But Lean UX designers embrace it as part of the process.

SHIFT: From BDUF to Agile-fall: same thing, new day

In the Agile community, you sometimes hear people talk about Big Design Up Front, or BDUF. We've been advocating moving away from BDUF for years. But it wasn't always that way.

In the early 2000s, Jeff was a user interface designer at AOL, working on a new browser. The team was working on coming up with ways to innovate on existing browser feature sets. But they always had to wait to implement anything until Jeff created the appropriate mockups, specifications, and flow diagrams that described these new ideas.

One developer got tired of waiting and started implementing some of these ideas before the documents were complete. Jeff was furious! How could he have gone ahead without design direction? How could he possibly know what to build? What if it was wrong or didn't work? He'd have to rewrite all the code!

Turns out the work he did allowed the team to see some of these ideas much sooner than before. It gave team members a glimpse into the actual product experience and allowed them to quickly iterate their designs to be more usable and feasible. From that moment on they relaxed the BDUF requirements, especially as the team pushed into features that required animations and new UI patterns.

The irony of the team's document-dependency and the "inspiration" it triggered in that one developer was not lost. In fact, at the end of the project, Jeff was given a mock award (Figure 8-1) for inspiring "undocumented creativity" in a teammate.

Figure 8-1. *Jeff's "award" for inspiring undocumented creativity in engineers*

Even though most teams these days actively shun the concept of Big Design Up Front, we've seen a resurgence in this practice in supposedly Agile environments. This new, sneaky version of BDUF is called *Agile-fall*. Agile-fall is the combination of an up-front design phase that results in work that is handed off, waterfall style, to an engineering team to then break up into stories and develop in an "agile" way. The argument for this way of working centers on the engineering team's desire to stay the course during implementation and to be able to predict when the work will ship with some degree of confidence. This is done in the name of predictability and efficiency.

The problem, of course, is that Agile-fall removes the collaboration between design and engineering that Lean UX requires to succeed. It ends up forcing teams to create big documentation to communicate design, followed by even lengthier negotiations between designers and developers. Sound familiar? It's BDUF in a new disguise. The waste created with Agile-fall is a symptom of a broader management issue that continues to push teams toward fixed scope and fixed deadlines. Engineers rightly feel the only way they can make scope and deadline commitments is if they have a crystal clear understanding of what needs to be developed, along with a promise that nothing will change. (Never mind that agile is about embracing change!) Of course, as we know by now, software is complex and unpredictable and, even with a locked-down design, the ability to predict exactly what will ship and when it will ship is closer to fortune-telling than it is to project management.

If Agile-fall is the way your team works, consider amplifying the conversation about managing to outcomes with your stakeholders. By moving the conversation away from fixed time and scope, and steering toward customer behavior as a measure of success, the demands to do all the design work up front should begin to disappear.

SHIFT: Speed first, aesthetics second

Jason Fried, CEO of Basecamp once said, "Speed first, aesthetics second."

He wasn't talking about compromising quality. He was talking about editing his ideas and process down to the core. In Lean UX, working quickly means generating many artifacts. Don't waste time debating which type of artifact to create, and don't waste time polishing them to perfection. Instead ask yourself the following:

- Who do I need to communicate with?
- What do I need to get across to them immediately?
- What's the least amount of work I need to do to communicate that to them?

If you're working with a developer who is sitting next to you, a whiteboard sketch might suffice. If an executive is asking detailed product questions, you might need to create a visual mockup. Customers might require prototypes. Whatever the scenario, create the artifact that will take the least amount of time. Remember, these artifacts are a transient part of the project—like a conversation. Get it done. Get it out there. Discuss. Move on.

Aesthetics—in the visual design sense—are an essential part of a finished product and experience. The fit and finish of these elements make a critical contribution to brand, emotional experience, and professionalism. At the visual design refinement stage of the process, putting the effort to obsess over this layer of presentation makes a lot of sense. However, putting in this level of polish and effort into the early-stage artifacts—wireframes, site maps, workflow diagrams—is (usually) a waste of time.

By sacrificing the perfection of intermediate design artifacts, your team will get to market faster, and learn more quickly which elements of the whole experience (design, workflow, copy, content, performance, value propositions, etc.) are working for the users and which aren't. And, you'll be more willing to change and rework your ideas if you've put less effort into presenting them.

SHIFT: Fall in love with the problem, not the solution

Lean UX makes us ask hard questions about the nature of quality in our design work.

If you're a designer reading this, you've probably asked yourself a question that often comes up when speed trumps aesthetic perfection:

> If my job is now to put out concepts and ideas instead of finished work, everything I produce will feel half-assed. I feel like I'm "going for the bronze." Nothing I produce will ever be finished. Nothing is indicative of the kind of products I am capable of designing. How can I feel pride and ownership for designs that are simply not done?

For some designers, Lean UX threatens what they value in their work and puts their portfolio at risk. It might even feel as though it threatens their future employability. These emotions are based on what many hiring managers have valued to date—sexy deliverables (i.e., solutions). Rough sketches, "version one" of a project, and other low-fidelity artifacts are not the making of a "killer portfolio." With the realization that software solutions continue to evolve over time, all of that is now changing.

Although your organization must continue to value aesthetics, polish, and attention to detail, other dimensions of design are equally important. The ability to understand the context of a business problem, think fast, and build shared understanding needs to get a promotion. Designers can demonstrate their problem-solving skills by illustrating the paths they took to get from idea to validated learning to experience. In doing so, they'll demonstrate their deep worth as designers. Organizations that seek out and reward problem-solvers will attract—and be attracted to—these designers.

Shift: UX debt

It's often the case that teams working in Agile processes do not actually go back to improve the user interface of the software. But as our friend Jeff Patton likes to say, "It's not iteration if you do it only once." Teams need to make a commitment to continuous improvement, and that means not simply refactoring code and addressing technical debt, it also means reworking and improving user interfaces. Teams need to embrace the concept of *UX debt* and make a commitment to continuous improvement of the user experience.

James O'Brien, an interaction designer working in London, describes what happened when his team began tracking UX debt in the same manner that the team used to track technical debt. "The effect was dramatic. Once we presented [rework] as debt all opposition fell away. Not only was there no question of the debt not being paid down, but it was consistently prioritized."

To begin tracking UX debt, you can just create a category of stories in your backlog called UX debt. Sometimes, though, experience problems are not something that a single team can solve—solving bigger problems can require the coordinated effort of many teams. For these larger efforts—experience problems that span large user journeys—try this:

- Create a customer journey map of the current experience
- Work together with your team to create a second journey map that shows the ideal experience
- Make these two artifacts clearly visible (on a wall) next to each other
- Identify teams responsible for portions of that customer journey and invite them to the wall to review the gap between current and desired states
- Work with these teams to write UX debt stories to go on their backlogs
- Clearly identify on the journey maps when the current experience has been improved and who is working on other improvements

SHIFT: Agencies are in the deliverables business

Applying Lean UX in an interactive agency is no small challenge. Most agencies have a business model that conflicts with Lean UX. The traditional agency business model is simple: clients pay for deliverables—designs, specs, code, PowerPoint decks—not outcomes. But agency culture is also a huge obstacle. The culture of hero design is strong in places that elevate individuals to positions like executive creative director. Cross-disciplinary collaboration can also be difficult in big agencies, where the need to keep utilization high has led to processes that encourage functional silos. These, in turn, lead to "project phases" that encourage deliverable-centric work.

Perhaps the most challenging obstacle is the client's expectation to "throw it over the wall" to the agency, and then see the results when they're ready. Collaboration between client and agency in this case can be limited to uninformed and unproductive critique that is based on personal bias, politics, and asscovering.

To make Lean UX work in an agency, everyone involved in an engagement must focus on maximizing two factors: increasing collaboration between client and agency, and working to change the focus from outputs to outcomes.

Some agencies are attempting to focus on outcomes by experimenting with a move away from fixed-scope and deliverable-based contracts. Instead, their engagements are based on simple time-and-materials agreements or, more radically, toward outcome-based contracts. In either case, the team becomes freer to spend its time iterating toward a specified goal. Clients give up the illusion of control that a deliverables-based contract offers but gain a freedom to pursue meaningful and high-quality solutions that are defined in terms of outcomes, not feature lists.

To increase collaboration, agencies can try to break down the walls that separate them from their clients. Clients can be pulled into the process earlier and more frequently. Check-ins can be constructed around less formal milestones. And collaborative work sessions can be arranged so that both agency and client benefit from the additional insight, feedback, and collaboration with each other.

These are not easy transformations—neither for the agency nor the client who hires them—but it is the model under which the best products are built.

A quick note about development partners

In agency relationships, software development teams (either at the agency, at the client, or a third-party team) are often treated as outsiders and often brought in at the end of a design phase. It's imperative that you change this: development partners must participate through the life of the project—not simply by including them as passive observers. Instead, you should seek to have software development begin as early as possible. Again, you are looking to create a deep and meaningful collaboration with the entire project team—and to do that, you must actually be working side by side with the developers.

In Chapter 9 we highlight two agencies, ustwo and Hello Group, that have found different paths for addressing these challenges.

SHIFT: Working with third-party vendors

Third-party software development vendors pose a big challenge to Lean UX methods. If a portion of your work is outsourced to a third-party vendor—regardless of the location of the vendor—the Lean UX process is more likely to break down. This is because the contractual relationship with these vendors can make the flexibility that Lean UX requires difficult to achieve.

When working with third-party vendors, try to create projects based on time and materials. This will make it possible for you to create a flexible relationship with your development partner. You will need this in order to respond to the changes that are part of the Lean UX process. Remember, you are building software to learn, and that learning will cause your plans to change. Plan for that change and structure your vendor relationships around it.

When selecting partners, remember that many outsourced development shops are oriented toward production work and see rework as a problem rather than a learning opportunity. When seeking partners for Lean UX work, look for teams willing to embrace experimentation and iteration, and who clearly understand the difference between prototyping-to-learn and developing-for-production.

SHIFT: Documentation standards

Depending on the domain you work in, your organization might impose strict documentation standards that meet both internal and regulatory compliance. These documents might not add any value for the project while it's in flight, yet the team still has to create them. Many teams struggle to move their projects forward when faced with these regulations. They wait until the documents are complete before beginning the design and implementation of the work slowing, down progress and team learning. Then, when the documents are complete, any adjustment of the work described within them is discouraged because of the documentation overhead that change drives.

This situation is exactly where, as designer and coach Lane Halley put it, you "lead with conversation, and trail with documentation." The basic philosophies and concepts of Lean UX can be executed within these environments—conversation, collaborative problem solving, sketching, experimentation, and so on—during the early parts of the project lifecycle. As hypotheses are proven and design directions solidify, transition from informal documentation practices back to the documentation standard your company requires. Use this documentation for the exact reason your company demands—to capture decision history and inform future teams working on this product. Don't let it hold you up from making the right product decisions.

SHIFT: Be realistic about your environment

Change is scary. The Lean UX approach brings with it a lot of change. This can be especially disconcerting for managers who have been in their position for a while and are comfortable in their current role. Some managers can be threatened by proposals to work in a new way—which could end up having negative consequences for you. In these situations, try asking for forgiveness rather than permission. Try out some ideas and prove their value with quantifiable success. Whether you saved time and money on the project or put out a more successful update than ever before—these achievements can help make your case. If your manager still doesn't see the value in working this way and you believe your organization is progressing down a path of continued "blind design," perhaps it's time to consider alternative employment.

SHIFT: Managing up and out

Lean UX gives teams a lot of freedom to pursue effective solutions. It does this by stepping away from a feature roadmap approach, and instead empowers teams to discover the features they think will best serve the business. But abandoning the feature roadmap has a cost—it removes a key tool that the business uses to coordinate the activity of teams. So, with the freedom to pursue your agenda comes a responsibility to communicate that agenda.

You must constantly reach out to members of your organization who are not currently involved in your work to make them aware of what's coming down the pike. This communication will also make you aware of what others are planning and help you to coordinate. Customer service managers, marketers, parallel business units, and sales teams all benefit from knowing what the product organization is up to. By reaching out to them proactively, you allow them to do their jobs better. In turn, they will be far less resistant to the change your product designs are making.

Here are two valuable lessons to ensure smoother validation cycles:

- There are always other departments who are affected by your work. Ignore them at your peril.
- Ensure customers are aware of any significant upcoming changes and provide them the option to opt out (at least temporarily).

Wrapping Up

In this chapter, we described some of the organizational shifts you'll probably be faced with as you implement Lean UX. In the next chapter, we look at some case studies of companies that are putting these ideas in motion, experiencing the shifts, and developing Lean UX ideas in the wild.

CHAPTER 9

Case Studies

*If you're not failing every now and again, it's a
sign you're not doing anything very innovative.*
—**Woody Allen**

In the previous chapter, you looked at some of the shifts that organizations
must make in order to begin working in a Lean UX style. In this chapter, we
share with you some case studies that illustrate how companies across industries are making these shifts. As you read, you'll see themes from Chapter 8
coming up. You'll also see organizations making compromises, balancing old
and new imperatives, and working to continuously adapt their processes, all
the while using Lean UX principles and methods as their guides.

Regulations and Financial Services: Lean UX at PayPal

Industry regulation presents a challenge for Lean UX. Lean UX teams like to
move quickly, to experiment with both process and product, to try new things,
and learn from failure. In regulated industries, however, failure isn't regarded
casually. Regulation usually exists to prevent failures and/or limit the damage
that failure can cause. Still, Lean approaches can work in regulated environments—it's all about figuring out how to experiment safely. This case study
shows how one team at PayPal began their Lean UX journey.

As one of the main forms of digital payment in the world, PayPal is ubiquitous
on the Internet. But unlike many Internet companies, PayPal works with
money. This means that all their work must run through a thorough legal, risk,
and regulatory compliance process. Is it possible to build and run regular

experiments in this context? Can it be done with a complicated organizational structure and multiple stakeholders? The Hermes project proved that it could.

Fixing Checkout

In 2012, PayPal's checkout process was stuck in the late 1990s, and the company was feeling the pinch. Complaints from customers were growing. Fast-growing startups like Square and Stripe threatened to drive down the payment giant's market share. PayPal's new President, David Marcus, who came from the startup world, saw an opportunity. Marcus wanted to reinvent Checkout, PayPal's core workflow. He appointed industry veteran Bill Scott to run the project that became known as the Hermes project. His mission: to modernize the primary way in which online customers bought products and services with PayPal.

At that point at PayPal, a project of this magnitude would require a massive team and a timeline counted in years, not months or weeks. *Marcus gave Scott six weeks to get it done.* To help move it along, Marcus also gave the team his Balsamiq-created sketches for what the experience should entail. For Scott, a PayPal newcomer, one thing was clear: he would need to find a new way for PayPal to work. Needless to say this was an intimidating proposition.

The Team

The first item on the agenda was staffing. Scott, working with the product and design organization, gathered a core cross-functional team of eight people. This team of product managers, designers, and engineers was astonishingly small by PayPal standards at that time. A typical PayPal project then would have involved dozens of individuals and multiple locations.

All eight team members were staffed out of the same office except one—the designer (who commuted regularly by plane to be with the team in San Jose, California). With only six weeks to get the work done, there was no time for emails, product requirements documents, conference calls, and the delays that come from working across multiple sites and multiple time zones.

To ensure that their ideas met with risk and compliance guidelines the team augmented their staff, when needed, with representatives from those practices. Working with risk and compliance people throughout the project was important: this practice alone saved the team weeks of effort. On a normal project, teams wouldn't meet with compliance until the end of the project. This big-batch approach to compliance caused delays and typically forced a flurry of last-minute product changes. The Hermes team, facing a looming deadline, couldn't risk that kind of late-stage delay.

Getting Started and Overcoming Obstacles

Setting up shop in the nicest conference room on campus, the team spent their first week throwing out their best ideas, sketching, and coming up with an initial set of hypotheses. They then decided on a rhythm for the rest of their activities. The team settled on a schedule of designing and building on Monday through Wednesday, testing with users on Thursdays, and reflecting and planning on Fridays.

The first couple of weeks felt productive. Engineers took advantage of existing APIs that moved real money, designers sketched on the whiteboards, and front-end developers connected the pieces by implementing the work directly from the whiteboard. There were regular check-ins on status and the team built momentum and shared understanding.

Then, about four weeks into the project the designers revolted. Sharing their work constantly on the whiteboard and receiving ongoing feedback and critique from their colleagues began to feel like design by committee. "When can we go and ideate on our own for a bit?" they wondered. The team realized that just throwing a cross-functional array of professionals together in one room, although a good start, was not enough to build productive collaboration. The team needed to rethink *how* it worked and not just *what* it was doing.

The designers wanted to avoid what the team came to call "pissing on the Picasso," a situation in which engineers respond to pixel-perfect mockups by debating what they can and can't implement. The team refined their process to ensure that designers got some time to refine their thinking. They learned when to create sketches collaboratively and when to create and present pixel-perfect mockups. They figured out how to get thinking time, and at the same time, avoid going too long without broader team feedback. Over time, the Hermes team found their rhythm and shipped the first iteration successfully.

The Results

The Hermes team redefined the process of building products at PayPal. They created a model that the company could use to move away from silos, geographically distributed staffing, and lengthy debates and approval processes. By including previously excluded colleagues in their process, they redefined the way teams work with regulatory and risk to continue to ensure that they didn't expose the company in a negative manner. The tweaks the team made to their design process allowed high-quality work to ship with less pushback from engineers. Finally, the things the Hermes engineering team learned laid the foundation for redesigning their tech stack to allow the rest of the organization to begin working with similar speed from prototype to production.

PayPal's new standard practice is based on the Hermes model: it builds full-stack teams that are self-sufficient, colocated (or at least in the same time zone), and focused on rapid delivery and learning cycles.

The product the team created with this Lean approach was also a tremendous business success for PayPal. It became the core of their new checkout experience, which drove measurably higher customer success rates for sellers and buyers.

Online to Offline: Lean UX at CarMax

For companies that offer a purely digital service, Lean UX practice can be fairly straightforward. They avoid many of the tangles created by real-world interactions and bricks-and-mortar commerce. But what happens when you're creating a multichannel service? This is the case at CarMax, a retailer that uses their online channel to drive people to their physical stores. How do you know your online service is working? How do you optimize an experience that involves online shopping, onsite browsing, and the integration of a large in-store sales force? This is exactly the challenge that CarMax faces on a daily basis.

As the largest used car retailer in the United States and a Fortune 500 company, CarMax relies heavily on both its website to inform and educate its customers about its inventory as well as its retail stores (160 of them and growing every month) to complete the actual sale.

Seeking an Outcome

In car sales, financing the purchase of the car is a critical component of the process.

CarMax wanted to optimize the online channel to ensure that customers who arrive at the store are not only educated but qualified and ready to buy. Could they do it? Archie Miller, UX designer, and Beth Sutherland, product manager, told us how their team discovered the answer.

The product team hypothesized that if customers better understood the financing side of purchasing a car, those customers would have a more successful car-buying experience when they arrived at the CarMax store. This project framing, seeking *outcomes* rather than committing to *outputs*, is at the heart of the Lean UX approach.

Lean UX + Customer Experience + Service Design

The team began its research by creating a customer journey map. To validate their thinking, they asked existing customers to create their own journey maps. CarMax's journey map had 80 steps. The customer-created journey map had eight. This was a big insight: the customers' world view was far less complex than the team had hypothesized.

Proto Personas

The biggest "A-ha!" moment this exercise revealed, though, had to do with how customers began their car-buying process. The exercise revealed a clear set of categories of factors that drove consumers into the car-buying process. For example, one persona that emerged (they called her Tiffany) was thrown into car buying through an unexpected life event like her car breaking down. The team felt this was an underserved segment.

They created other personas, as well, and they further validated these personas with a series of conversations CarMax ran using Ethnio to intercept shoppers on their website and engage in dialog. (Overall, the team spoke with more than 100 car shoppers to confirm these new findings.)

In addition, they learned two more important consumer insights about this group of customers:

- Most customers who fell into this category did not enjoy the car-buying process.
- Many of these shoppers faced a confidence gap about whether they would be approved for financing to purchase a CarMax vehicle.

Many people knew their overall credit profile, but didn't know what it would mean for their ability to be approved for a loan. In their words, "Do I even qualify for a car loan with CarMax?"

The team set out to help their customers feel comfortable during their car-buying experience and ensure that they made the best purchase for their needs and budget while at the same time helping the business achieve its goals. The team began by creating *empathy maps* during each contextual interview with a customer. This helped team members realize insights and recognize consumer behavior patterns.

Figure 9-1. *Empathy maps that the entire team created during customer interviews*

Testing a Hypothesis

One of the first things the team wanted to test was whether the shortest loan application form would increase completion rates. They mocked up an initial draft in Axure, which you can see in Figure 9-2.

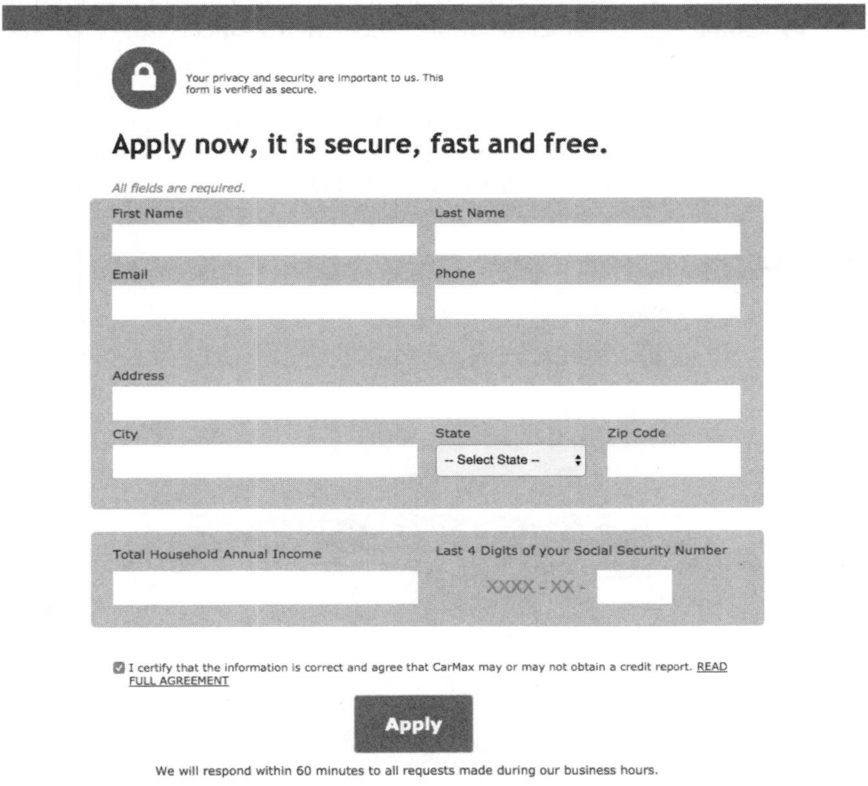

Apply now, it is secure, fast and free.

Your privacy and security are important to us. This form is verified as secure.

All fields are required.

First Name | Last Name

Email | Phone

Address

City | State -- Select State -- | Zip Code

Total Household Annual Income | Last 4 Digits of your Social Security Number
XXXX - XX -

☑ I certify that the information is correct and agree that CarMax may or may not obtain a credit report. READ FULL AGREEMENT

Apply

We will respond within 60 minutes to all requests made during our business hours.

Figure 9-2. *The first form the team created—the shortest possible form—in Axure*

Using Ethnio to get users to work through their prototype, the team was surprised to learn that a short form, albeit simple and quick to complete, didn't give users a sense of confidence that they were actually approved for a loan. This led many of the participants to believe that when they got to the store they'd have to go through loan approval again. These customers actually wanted to provide *more* information so that it "felt more like a loan application" than the prototype led them to believe.

The Next Iteration

The team set out to design a longer form with the internal challenge to not make it "feel" like a long form. Having a good sense of "Tiffany" and her needs, the team decided that a budget calculator was a good place to begin. This would allow Tiffany to determine whether she could afford the monthly car payment. This was followed by asking for the remaining information necessary to complete a credit application. These two elements together would reveal whether customers qualified for a loan, making the rest of the form process relevant or, in some cases, not worth the extra effort. Again, the team went to Ethnio and Axure to create and test the form. The end result (see Figure 9-3) was a "chunked-up" long form—a higher number of fields broken down into categories—that didn't feel as long. Figure 9-4 shows the actual finished form.

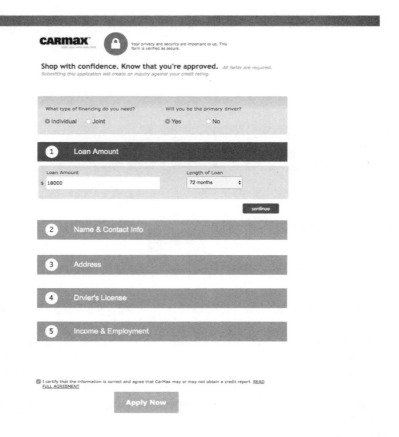

Figure 9-3. *The "long and chunked-up" prototype form that the team created in Axure*

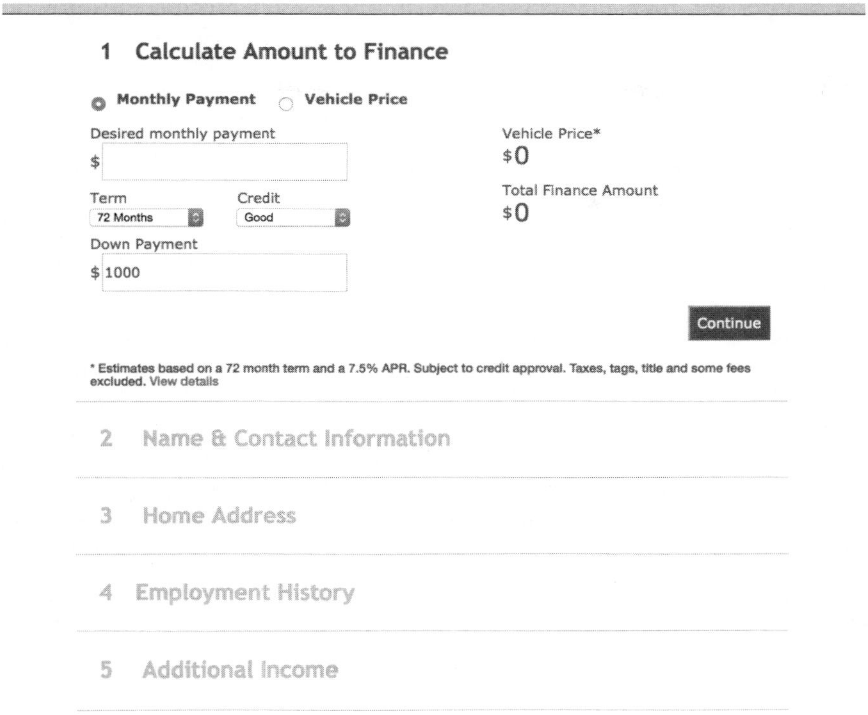
1 Calculate Amount to Finance
Monthly Payment
Vehicle Price
Desired monthly payment
$
Vehicle Price*
$0
Total Finance Amount
$0
Term
72 Months
Credit
Good
Down Payment
$ 1000
Continue
* Estimates based on a 72 month term and a 7.5% APR. Subject to credit approval. Taxes, tags, title and some fees excluded. View details
2 Name & Contact Information
3 Home Address
4 Employment History
5 Additional Income

Figure 9-4. *The first "live" form that shipped to real customers*

Testing Another Hypothesis

Sometimes, it makes sense to use your research process to test more than one question at a time. That's what the CarMax team did here. As the team refined their form design, they began testing a second hypothesis: would customers even *want* to be prequalified for a car loan before arriving at the store?

To answer this question, the team used a method called the "404 test" or "button to nowhere." In this case, the team placed call-to-action buttons to apply for a car loan in various places on their mobile website. Then, they watched traffic logs to see what the rate of response was for these calls to action.

Clicking the first implementation of the call to action displayed a "feature coming soon" message. It wasn't a great experience for the user, but it gave the team a good sense of where to put these elements and how best to word them. They refined the test to drive away from this "404-style page" toward a lead-generation form. This worked to both the users' benefit—making them feel like they were making progress in their application—and the team's—informing them on the best entry points for the loan application process and providing real customer data to executives to validate their design decisions.

Integrating In-Store Sales Staff

Including sales consultants from the beginning of the project allowed the product team to ensure that the design of the information being delivered to the store sales staff met their needs and allowed them to have more meaningful conversations with customers either on the phone or when they arrived at the store. For sales consultants in the stores these new loan applications provided a way to understand customers' needs more effectively.

The team observed sales consultants at two different stores to understand how they used this information. The team came to understand what information was useful at various points of the customer interaction, and this helped them design the way the information was presented to sales people. Initially, the team's new loan application presented information on a "decisions page." This assumed that the customer had already selected a car. In reality, neither the sales consultant nor the customer were at that phase yet. The feedback from the store staff allowed the team to iterate their information design to be more in sync with the actual sales process.

By iterating and testing different ways to present the information for their sales colleagues, the team found the right combination of information and design to shift these conversations from "What kind of car would you like?"—a question many buyers don't really have an answer for—to, "Let's discuss the kind of cars you qualify for"—which is a far more productive conversation for both parties.

Regular Cadence with the Team

This project was a textbook example of a balanced team sharing the Lean UX work. Research sessions were scheduled consistently on the same day (Thursday) every week and invitations extended to the entire product team. Between each session, the team would stay engaged by conducting sketching sessions to refine the prototype and the testing script.

In addition, the team proactively communicated to colleagues through a variety of channels. They posted all of their findings on wall space in the office where many of their colleagues could see it. The team took advantage of CarMax's culture of storytelling by creating the concept of "open houses" conducted by various product teams, as demonstrated in Figure 9-5. These public space events showcased a team's work and allowed executives as well as other teams to get a sense of how projects were progressing, what was working, and what the team was shifting based on its learning.

Figure 9-5. *Miller (closest to the board on the left) and Sutherland (right) sharing their findings at an open-house event*

Setting Client Expectations at a Digital Product Studio: Lean UX at ustwo

There are many challenges when it comes to selling product development consulting. By definition, you're trying to create something from nothing, so ambiguity and uncertainty are high. In this context, getting aligned on project scope and working process is critical. Add a new, unfamiliar process like Lean UX and things become even more complicated. In this case study, we look at how ustwo, a consulting firm with studios in London, New York, Malmö, and Sydney, has addressed this challenge.

There are lots of challenges at the beginning of a consulting engagement. You need to build a shared understanding of the goals of the engagement with your client. You need to set the appropriate expectations about what the agency is committed to achieving. You must ensure that your client understands how you plan to work and how you expect to collaborate. Finally, if you're working in a Lean UX approach, you need to help your client understand and commit to a more outcome-driven result (rather than the more typical approach in which you agree to build a specific predefined set of features). Design studio ustwo has created and refined an approach to tackling these challenges head on.

The Service Definition Workshop

ustwo has created a short preengagement phase they call a *Service Definition Workshop*. They sell this to every client *before* they commit to taking on the entire project. This workshop involves the team that will work on the full project and key stakeholders from the client. They spend one to two days together to lay out the assumptions of the project, the risks that are involved, what skills they'll need, and what kind of support will be required from the client.

Using a series of facilitated brainstorming exercises, convergent and divergent thinking explorations, and affinity mapping techniques, ustwo introduces the concepts of Lean UX to the client, sets expectations about how much client participation will be necessary in the full project, and begins the trust-building process.

The Service Definition Workshop sets the scope of the work and expectations for how the team will address the work. It allows the newly formed client/ agency team to create the following:

- A shared understanding of the vision and goal of the project
- A prioritized list of business goals
- A clear sense of who the first users of the system will be
- A proposed customer journey for those users
- An initial set of desired features that the team feels are important

The team captures their learning on a single-page canvas, as shown in Figure 9-6.

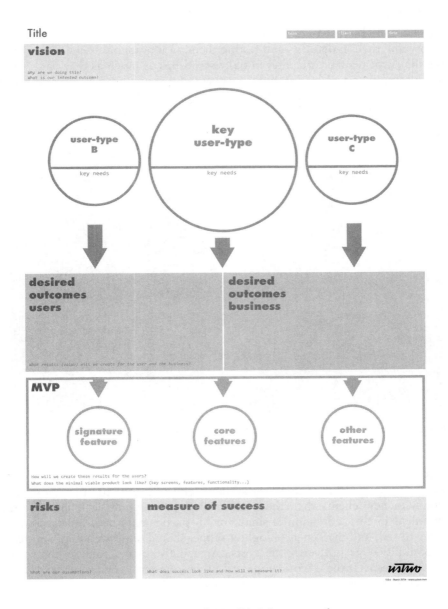

Figure 9-6. *The Service Definition Workshop canvas from ustwo*

Following the Workshop, MVPs and Collaboration

After the initial two-day collaboration, ustwo spent an additional two weeks prototyping their early ideas and testing them with potential users. During this time the client team participates in daily stand-ups as much as they can. When the prototyping phase is over, both the client and ustwo have a clearer sense of what the project will entail, what the scope of that effort might be, and, perhaps most important, what it's going to be like to work together.

Figure 9-7. *ustwo team members and their client participating in a Service Definition Workshop*

ustwo have found this fixed-price engagement (in many ways a variation of the Design Sprint technique) to be a far more effective way to share how they work with new clients than the traditional Keynote pitch deck. Because the investment in this workshop is small for all participants it's a relatively easy service to sell, and the benefits—tighter scope, shared understanding, and team compatibility—far outweigh the costs. Amazingly, ustwo told us that more than 50 percent of these workshops end up in long-term engagements, a much better close rate than they see with their traditional pitches.

Lean UX in an Agency: Changing the Way We Sell Work

Lean UX grew up in the context of digital product development and the process changes required to thrive in the digital age. Companies that grew successful in predigital times built processes that made sense then but might have outlived their usefulness. Changing processes to become more digital can be difficult. This is especially true for advertising agencies that grew up around the production processes of the print and broadcast world. In this case study, we'll look at how one successful marketing agency, Hello Group, is adapting to a digital world.

Hello Group, a growing digital agency with its roots in advertising, has been transitioning into broader design and strategy work for the past few years. As part of that, the agency had to rethink the way they partner with clients and third-party engineering vendors to deliver work. Lean UX has played a pivotal role in shifting the way they work. The company has drawn inspiration from Lean UX to create two important new tools to help them shape that conversation with their clients, vendors, and within the agency, with their own management team, as well.

Alignment, Coordination, and Flexibility

One big problem Hello Group faced was how to articulate the scope of their project work to the client and their engineering vendors in a way that created alignment and understanding but also provided enough flexibility to allow them to explore different features and alternative design implementations. Using the Lean UX hypothesis as a model, the agency created a tool called the *Experience Story*.

Experience Stories are mini-scenario statements that ensure designers stay focused on solving the problem at hand without becoming lost in the minutiae of feature details. It helps the design team stay focused on the vision, something that can so often become lost in the day-to-day micromanagement of tasks and progress. Experience Stories are based on customer research and observation insights. They describe the ideal experience a customer should go through when engaging with a service. They're made up of three parts:

- The current situation with which the customer is faced
- The friction involved in that situation that the team is trying to address
- The ideal experience the team wants to create

Here's an example:

> Two days on the cruise ship is a time filled with experiences. Guests come on board with the expectation of making the best of this time.
>
> But we demand a lot from our guests; remember to print your boarding pass; remember which card was for breakfast and which was for dinner; remember whether you've paid for the dinner, etc.
>
> A good experience would be when all of these details disappear and guests flow through the cruise ship from check in to check out.

These Experience Stories are shared both internally and with Hello's clients and partners. This helps everyone orient around *why* the project is important and it serves as a consistent yardstick for all of the parties on a project.

Working with Third-Party Engineers

A second and perhaps even more daunting challenge Hello Group faced was their reliance on third-party engineering vendors to build the designs Hello Group created. If Hello wanted to work in a Lean UX way, how could they ensure that their partners—who are hired and incentivized differently—would conform to this way of working? They decided to use something they call the *Project Working Agreement*.

Inspired by David Bland's *Team Working Agreement*, the Project Working Agreement lays out, in very clear terms, exactly how the different agencies will work together.[1] The agreement covers things like the following:

- What flavor of Agile the agencies will use
- How long sprints are
- Where the code will be kept
- When the teams will meet
- What tools they'll use to meet and communicate

And much more.

It might seem like a lengthy, tedious exercise with which to kick off a project, but it's proven to save Hello hours of negotiation later in the project. Figure 9-8 shows what it looks like.

---

1 You can find a copy of this at *http://www.leanuxbook.com/links.*

Hello Project Agreement

A document that in two parts describes how we want to work with the client and potential 3rd party vendor.
The project agreement should be filled out at the start of a project and reviewed throughout the project if needed.

Part I - Process

Process Overview	
Agile Process Style	
Sprint Length	

Ceremonies		
Stand Up		Location:
Sprint Planning Meetings		Location:
Sprint Review		Location:
Retrospectives with client		Location:
PM status meetings		Location:
User validation		Responsible:

Working Hours	
Team Work Day	

Product owner & back-log	
Product owner	
Back-log owner	
Back-log format	
Prioritisation of back-log	
Writer of hypotheses writer	
Writer of experience stories + job stories	
Writer of development user stories	
Definition of done	

Communication/Tools	
Project Discussion	
Document Sharing	
Story Management	
Design sharing	
Development tool	

Deliverables		
UX		Language:
Design		Language:
Copy		Language:
Transition design		Language:
Code structure		

Development	
Supported browsers/OS/devices	
Testing expectations	
Test responsible	
Release intervals	
Code version control	
Merge Policy	
Level of specifications	

Deployment	
Acceptance	
Deployed by	
Technical tests	

Scope changes	
Process for scope changes	

Additional document to be filled out: Roles and responsibilities sheet

Figure 9-8. *The template that Hello Group uses to capture the Project Working Agreement*

The Project Working Agreement is a tool for improving collaboration, something that is of paramount importance in Lean UX. And, like most things at the start of a project, the agreement is based on a series of assumptions. As a result, Hello Group treats the agreement as a living document. As the project progresses, the efficacy of the tactics listed in the agreement will vary. Teams can decide to update the agreement as needed in order to make the working process more productive.

A Last Word

Sometimes, it can feel impossible to change the entrenched habits of an organization. So, we were delighted to receive this email from our colleague Emily Holmes. As we read it, we knew we had to share it with you.

In the email, Emily, who is Director of UX at Hobsons, an educational-technology company in the Washington, DC, area, details the changes she's made in her organization. Here are some excerpts that describe the journey her firm has taken:

> I think a lot of enterprise companies struggle to figure out the best way to implement these techniques. We initially got a great deal of resistance that we couldn't do Lean UX because we're "not a startup," but of course that's really not true.
>
> We brought in a coach to help reinforce with the team our goal of moving our development process toward a Lean UX methodology (it can help to have an outside voice to reinforce what's being said internally), and since then we've made good progress. In less than a year, our team structure has moved from this:

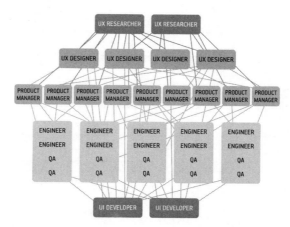

Figure 9-9. *Hobson's original team structure*

To this:

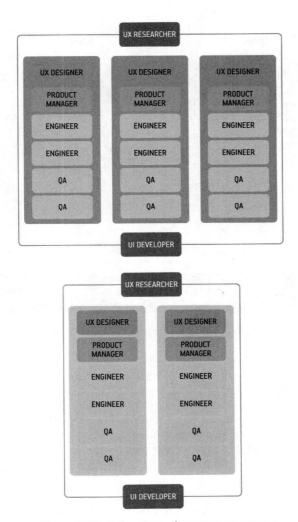

Figure 9-10. *Hobson's new lean team structure*

I have introduced the following process/system for helping our teams internalize what needs to happen as we move through the discovery phase of a project, so we don't skip any steps and so everyone can begin understanding why this thought process needs to happen.

Figure 9-11. *Emily Holmes's Lean UX "game" diagram*

It requires ongoing coaching on my part and we haven't completely mastered it yet, but it is really helping to get the full team in sync and speaking the same language. That's no small feat, since our team includes people who are accustomed to business analysis, technical specs and waterfall development. It's a little bit fun, so people don't feel too resentful about having to change old habits. And, it definitely helps us fight the "monsters" that have traditionally been problematic for our organization.

I believe a lot of the things that are working for us could be applied to other enterprise organizations quite successfully.

We believe that, too, and hope the stories we've presented in this chapter will help to inspire you on your Lean UX journey.

Index

A

A/B testing, 91, 111
AARRR (Startup Metrics for Pirates), 34
"Adapting Usability Investigations for Agile User-centered Design", 120
aesthetics, 147
affinity mapping exercise, 69
agencies
    changing the way they sell work, lean UX case study, 167-170
    deliverables and, 148
    development partners and, 149
Agile software development, 4, 8
    integrating Lean UX with, 117-136
    case study, Knowsy, 129-133
    communicating with stakeholders, 133
    definition of Agile terms, 118
    dual-track Agile, 123
    in the enterprise, 134
    participation in processes, 128
    staggered sprints and modern off-shoots, 120
    using Scrum to build lean UX practice, 125-128
    tools for improving collaboration, 71
    user stories versus hypotheses, 44
Agile-fall, 146
analysis versus making, 16

analytics, site usage, 111
Apple, Human Interface Guidelines (HIG), 60
asset libraries, 60
assumptions, 22-29
    declaring, 24
        preparation for, 25
        problem statement, 25
        who to involve, 24
        running business assumptions exercise, 28
        turning into hypothesis statement, 30
        types of, important to lean UX, 24
Axure, 108

B

backlogs, 118
    in dual-track Agile, 123
Balsamiq, 93
batches, working in, 15
BDUF (big design up front), shifting away from, 144
behavior, measuring (with MVPs), 78
behavioral infomation (personas), 37
Bezos, Jeff, 142
big design up fron (BDUF), shifting from, 144
Blank, Steve, 15
Bootstrap framework, 62

brand guidelines, 60
Brown, Tim, 8
build-measure-learn feedback loop, 9
business assumptions exercise, 28
business outcomes, 24, 32
  (see also outcomes)
  brainstorming possible outcomes, 32

C

Cagan, Marty, 123
  dual-track Agile process diagram, 123
CarMax, lean UX at (case study),
  156-163
  integrating in-store sales staff, 162
  lean UX, customer experience, and
    service design, 157
  next iteration of finance application,
    160
  proto-personas, 157
  seeking an outcome, 156
  testing a hypothesis, 159
  testing another hypothesis, 161
case studies, 153-172
  lean UX in an agency, changing the
    way they sell work, 167-170
  online to offline, lean UX at CarMax,
    156-163
  regulations and financial services, lean
    UX at PayPal, 153-156
  setting client expectations at digital
    product studio, lean UX at ustwo,
    163-166
  team organization at Hobson,
    170-172
clickable mockups, 108
client expectations, setting at digital
  product studio, ustwo case study,
  163-166
code repositories, 60
coded and live-data prototypes, 90
  coded prototypes in usability testing,
    108
collaboration
  among distributed teams, 143
  breaking down physical barriers to,
    143
  in Lean UX, 5

  in Sy and Miller's staggered sprints
    model, 120
  making it work, 71
  organizational roles and, 140
collaborative design (see design)
collaborative discovery, 96
  example of, 98
  in the field, 97
colocated teams, benefits of, 11
communication services, real-time, 143
competencies over roles, 141
continuous discovery, 15
continuous integration, 4
conversation among team members, 51
copy writing styles, 68
cover your ass (CYA) behavior, 141
creativity, experimentation and, 14
cross-functional collaboration
  importance of, 142
  organizational roles and, 140
cross-functional teams, 11
  orgnizational shift to, 142
culture
  changing in implementing lean UX,
    138
    agency culture, 148
    being realistic about your environ-
      ment, 151
    falling in love with the problem,
      not the solution, 147
    humility, 139
    no more heroes, 144
    workspaces, 143
  lean UX principles guiding, 12
    moving from doubt to certainty, 12
    no rock stars, gurus, or ninjas, 13
    outcomes, not output, 12
    permission to fail, 13
    removing waste, 13
    shared understanding, 13
customer feedback
  getting from a prototype MVP, 93
  in continuous discovery, 15
  in lean startup, 9
  on-site feedback surveys, 110
  teams getting, 11
customer journey maps, 148, 157

customer service, harnessing their knowledge, 109
customers
    AARRR in Startup Metrics for Pirates, 34
    determinations about, using proto-personas, 39

D

Dailey, Robert, 142
data-informed versus data-driven design, 30
dedicated teams, benefits of, 11
deliverables, 9
    agency culture and, 148
    focusing on outcomes instead of, 16
delivery backlog, 123
demographic information (personas), 37
demos and previews for prototypes, 92
deployment
    continuous, 4
    environments not allowing for frequent releases, 120
design
    collaborative, 47-74
        design systems, 58-68
        informal approach, 49
        making collaboration work, 71
        more structured approch, 51
        running a design studio, 52-57
        with geographically distributed teams, 68-71
    data-informed versus data-driven, 30
    Lean UX, 4
    of physical materials versus software, 3
    shifting from BDUF to Agile-fall, 144
    speed trumping aesthetic perfection, 147
    sprint zero or staggered sprints, 120
    user experience, 7
design sessions, 49
    collaborative, with distributed teams, 69
        priming the pump with affinity mapping, 69
        setup, 69

design sprints, 119, 120
    evolution of, 121
    kicking off themes with, 125
    pitfalls to watch out for, 122
design studios, running, 52
    individual idea generation, 53
    pairing up to iterate and refine, 56
    presentation and critique, 55
    problem definition and constraints, 53
    process, 52
    setting, 52
    supplies, 53
    team, 52
    team idea generation, 57
    using the output, 57
    with remote teams, 70
design systems, 58-68
    benefits of, 60
    case study, GE design system, 61-64
    clarifying terminology, 60
    creating, 64-68
        characteristics of successful design systems, 65
        elements included in design systems, 66
design thinking, 8
designers
    new skills for UX designers, 141
    participation in Agile processes, 128
    wanting to be heroes, 144
development partners
    participation in all phases of project lifecycle, 149
    working with third-party engineers, 168
    working with third-party vendors, 150
digital design systems (see design systems)
digital product studio, setting client expectations at, ustwo case study, 163-166
discovery
    in dual-track Agile, 124
    separate discovery and delivery teams, 124
discovery backlog, 123
    problems with, 124
discovery, collaborative (see collaborative discovery)

discovery, continuous (see continuous discovery)
distributed teams
  collaborating with, 68-71
  working with in lean UX implementation, 143
documentation standards, 150
doubt to certainty, moving from, 12
dual-track Agile, 119, 123

E

empathy maps, 157
empowered teams, 11
enterprise organizations
  implementing lean UX at, 170
  lean UX and Agile in, 134
Experience Stories, 167
experiment stories, 126
  elements contained in, 127
experimentation and creativity, 14
externalizing your work, 16

F

facilitation as core designer compentency, 141
failure, permission to fail, 13
feature fakes, 81
features, 24
  A/B testing, 91
  assembling your feature hypotheses, 42
  determining, exercise in, 41
  focusing on outcomes instead of, 21
  hypothesis statment focused on, 30
  stepping away from feature roadmap approach, 151
feedback, 95
  (see also customer feedback; research and learning)
  gaining market feedback with continuous deployment, 4
  in design studio presentation and critique, 55
file-sharing software, 143
Flickr, feature fakes, 82
Fried, Jason, 146

G

gated, handoff-based (waterfall) processes, avoiding, 11
GE design system (case study), 61-64
GEL design system, Westpac, 67
Goldstone, Lane, 129
GOOB (getting out of the building), 15
Google Hangouts, 68
Google Sheets, using in affinity mapping, 69
gurus, 13

H

hardcoded (or static data) prototypes, 91
Hello Group agency, changing the way they sell work (lean UX case study), 167-170
  alignment, coordination, and flexibility, 167
Hermes project, 154
heroes, shifting away from, 144
high-fidelity on-screen prototypes, 90
high-fidelity visual mockups (not clickable), 106
Hipchat, 143
HTML/CSS framework, Bootstrap, 62
Human Interface Guidelines (HIG), Apple, 60
human needs, identifying, 8
hypotheses, 22
  backlog of, from design sprints, 122
  for features, 42
  getting from problem statement to hypothesis, 31
    completing your hypothesis statements, 32
  hypothesis statements versus Agile user stories, 44
  prioritizing, 44
  tactical and testable, 30
  testing a hypothesis in CarMax case study, 159, 161
  transforming business assumptions into, 30
hypothesis statement, 22

I

impact, 34
implementation, understanding, creating an MVP for, 79
Industrial Internet Design System (IIDS), 62
interviews
collaborative discovery in the field, 97
planning questions for, 98
IPMs (see iteration planning meetings)
iteration planning meetings, 119, 126

J

JavaScript, Polymer framework, 63

K

key performance indicators (KPIs), 32
Kickstarter, landing page MVPs, 81
Knapp, Jake, 121
Knowsy case study, 129-133
breaking the design bottleneck, 132
outcome of Knowsy's foray into Lean UX, 133
shared vision empowering independent work, 131
The Innovation Games Company (TIGC), 130
Kowitz, Braden, 121

L

landing page tests, 81
LaunchRocket, 81
lean startup, 9
Lean UX, 4
components of, 5
defined, 10
integrating with Agile, 117-136
learning, 95
(see also research and learning)
continuous, 99-103
in the lab, three users each Thursday, 99
design sprints and, 122
learning goals for MVPs, 77, 77
being clear about, 79
Truth Curve, 80

understanding implementation, 79
understanding the value of your idea, 78
live-data prototypes, 91
low-fidelity on-screen mockups, 89

M

making, valuing over analysis, 16
management check-ins and team momentum, 133
MapMyRun, feature fake example, 84
McClure, Dave, 33
meetings (in Scrum), 125
Meetup, usability testing, three users every Thursday, 101
middle- and high-fidelity on-screen prototypes, 90
Miller, Lynn, 120
minimum viable products (MVPs), 9, 22, 75-87
creating, 77
guidelines for, 79
to understand implementation, 79
to understand value, 78
defined, 76
examples of, 81-87
deciding whether to launch a newsletter, 76
Wizard of Oz MVP for Taproot Plus, 85
in Meetup's mobile usability testing, 102
in ustwo lean UX case study, 166
using a prototype MVP, 92
monitoring techniques for continuous and collaborative discovery, 108-112
A/B testing, 111
customer service, 109
on-site feedback surveys, 110
search logs, 110
site usage analytics, 111
MVPs (see minimum viable products)

N

needs, obstacles, and desires (personas), 38
ninjas, 13

O

online to offline, lean UX at CarMax (case study), 156-163
organizational shifts in implementing lean UX, 137-151
  changing culture, 138
    being realistic about your environment, 151
    falling in love with the problem, not the solution, 147
    humility, 139
    no more heroes, 144
    shifting agency culture, 148
    workspaces, 143
  new skills for UX designers, 141
  outcomes, 140
  shifting process, 139
    doumentation standards, 150
    from BDUF to Agile-fall, 144
    managing up and out, 151
    UX debt, 148
  shifting team organization, 138
    cross-functional teams, 142
    distributed teams, 143
    roles and, 140
    working with third-party vendors, 150
organizations, benefits of design systems for, 61
outcomes
  driving vision with, 21-46
    assumptions, 23
    from problem statement to hypothesis, 31
    using the right words, 22
  managing to, with multiple teams in enterprises, 135
  not output, 12
  output, outcome, and impact, 34
  seeking in CarMax case study, 156
  shifting to, in implementing lean UX, 140, 148
output
  focusing on outcomes instead of, 12, 32
  output, outcome, and impact, 34
outsourcing
  of research, problems with, 96
  working with third-party vendors, 150

P

paper prototypes, 88
  in Knowsy case study, 132
  pros and cons of, 89
participants, recruiting for usability testing, 101
patterns
  finding in research data, 103
  identifying over time in lean UX research data, 104
Patton, Jeff, 123, 148
PayPal, lean UX at (case study), 153-156
  fixing checkout, 154
  getting started and overcoming obstacles, 155
  results of Hermes project, 155
  team, 154
permission to fail, 13
personas, 35
  considering in feature hypothesis construction, 43
  created in CarMax case study, 157
  creation process, 38
  developing in lean UX, 35
  sketching proto-personas on paper, 37
Polymer framework, 63
Predix design system, GE, 62
principles of lean UX, 7
  foundations, 7
    Agile software design, 8
    design thinking, 8
    lean startup, 9
    user experience design, 7
  guiding culture, 12
  guiding process, 14
  guiding team organization, 10
proactive communication, 133
problem statements, 25
  for existing products, 25
  for new products and services, 27
  getting from problem statement to hypothesis, 31
problem-focused teams, 11

falling in love with the problem, not the solution, 147

process

diagram of lean UX process, 22

lean UX principles guiding, 14

continuous discovery, 15

externalizing your work, 16

getting out of deliverables business, 16

GOOB, user-centricity, 15

valuing making over analysis, 16

working in small batches to mitigate risk, 15

shifting in implementing lean UX, 139

documentation standards, 150

from BDUF to Agile-fall, 144

from output to outcomes, 140

managing up and out, 151

speed first, aesthetics second, 146

UX debt, 148

product development consulting, lean UX at ustwo (case study), 163-166

product discovery, 119

Product IQ, raising for team members, 24

project working agreement, 168

proto-personas, 35

example of use, CSA project in NYC, 37

in CarMax case study, 157

prototypes, 88-93

choosing technique to use for, 88

coded and live-data prototypes, 90

demos and previews of, 92

elements included in, 91

example, using a prototype MVP, 92

low-fidelity on-screen mockups, 89

middle- and high-fidelity on-screen prototypes, 90

paper, 88

produced from design sprints, 121

prototyping tools, 88

R

real-time communication services, 143

recruiting participants for usability testing, 101

regulations and financial services, lean UX at PayPal, 153-156

remote-pairing software (Screenhero), 143

requirements, 22

research and learning, 95-112

continuous and collaborative research, 96

collaborative discovery, 96-98

continuous learning, 99-103

in the lab, three users each Thursday, 99

making research coninuous and collaborative, 95

making sense of the research data, 103-108

confusion, contradiction, and lack of clarity, 103

monitoring techniques for continuous and collaborative discovery, 108-112

scheduling of research sessions in CarMax case study, 162

retrospectives, 71

defined, 119

Ries, Eric, 9

risk mitigation, 23

risk prioritization matrix, 44

working in small batches, 15

rock stars, 13

"The Role of Team and Task Characteristics in R&D Team Collaborative Problem Solving and Productivity", 142

roles, moving from, to collaborative capabilities, 140

S

Salesforce design system, 66

Scrum, 117

defined, 118

using in building a lean UX practice, 125-128

experiment stories, 126

iteration planning meeting, 126

kicking off themes with a design sprint, 125

themes, 125

user validation schedule, 128
search logs, using for MVP validation, 110
self-sufficient teams, 11
shared understanding, 13
  proto-personas and, 36
short cycles, 4
site usage analytics, 111
Sivers, Derek, 14
six-up templates, 53
sketches, 105
sketching/ideation in design sprints, 125
Skype, 68
Skype in the classroom mockup example, 108
Slack, 68, 143
small teams
  benefits of, 11
  shifting to, in implementing lean UX, 142
SMS usage, research on, 104
software development vendors, third-party, 150
speed first, aesthetics second, 146
Sprint (Knapp, Zeratsky, and Kowitz), 121
sprint zero, 119
sprints, 118
  staggered sprints and modern off-shoots, 120
staggered sprints, 120
stakeholders
  proactive communication with, 134
  prototypes and, 88
stand-up, 118
"Startup Metrics for Pirates", 33
style guides, 60
  successful, characteristics of, 65
  wiki-based, 68
Sy, Desiree, 120

T

Taproot Foundation, Wizard of Oz MVP for, 85
team organization
  lean UX principles guiding, 10
  cross-functional teams, 11

problem-focused teams, 11
  self-sufficient and empowered teams, 11
  small, dedicated, colocated teams, 11
  shifting in implementing lean UX, 138
  cross-functional teams, 142
  Hobson education technology, 170-172
  small teams, 142
  working with distributed teams, 143
  working with third-party vendors, 150
Team Working Agreements, 72
team-based mentality, 13
teams
  benefits of design systems for, 61
  conversation among members, 51
  for design studio, 52
    idea generation by team, 57
  geographically distributed, collaborating with, 68-71
    collaborative design sessions, 69
  in enterprise organizations, 134
  in lean UX at Paypal case study, 154
  making collaboration work, 71
  management check-in and team momentum, 133
  participation of all members in Agile processes, 129
  raising Product IQ of members, 24
  separate discovery and delivery teams, 124
test-driven development (TDD), 22
testing
  simplifying the in-house test environment, 100
  test what you've got policy, 105
themes, 125
  kicking off with a design sprint, 125
third party vendors, working with, 150
  in Hello Group lean UX case study, 168
three, twelve, one activity calendar, 99
TIGC (The Innovation Games Company), 130
Trello board, using as a database, 85

Truth Curve (for MVPs), 80
two-pizza teams, 142

U

Unbounce, 81
understanding, shared, 13
    proto-personas and, 36
usability labs, 100
usability testing
    three users each Thursday at Meetup,
      101
    three users in the lab each Thursday,
      99-101
    watchers for the tests, 100
usage analytics, 111
user experience design, 7
    new skills for UX designers, 141
user outcomes, 24, 40
    features that help in achievement of,
      41
user stories (Agile), 118
    difference between hypotheses and, 44
    experiment stories and, 126
user-centered design, integrating with
    Agile, 120
user-centricity (GOOB), 15
users, 24
    in hypothesis statement exercise, 35
    personas, development of, 35
    remembering we are not the user, 37
    user validation schedule, 128
ustwo, lean UX at (case study), 163-166
    post-workshop MVPs and collabora-
      tion, 166

service definition workshop, 164
UX (user experience), 8, 47
UX debt, 148

V

value, understanding, creating an MVP
    for, 78
video conferencing software, 143
vision, driving with outcomes, 21-46
    assumptions, 23
      declaring, 24
        running business assumptions exer-
          cise, 28
    getting from problem statement to
      hypothesis, 31
    using the right words, 22

W

waste, removing, 13
    staggered sprints and, 121
waterfall processes, avoiding, 11
Web Components, 63
Westpac GEL design system, 67
"Why You Need to Fail" (video), 14
wiki-based style guides, 68
wireframes, 93
    in usability testing, 106
Wizard of Oz MVP, 84
work, externalizing, 16
workspaces, open and collaborative, 143

Z

Zeratsky, John, 121

Learn from experts.
Find the answers you need.

Sign up for a **10-day free trial** to get **unlimited access** to all of the content on Safari, including Learning Paths, interactive tutorials, and curated playlists that draw from thousands of ebooks and training videos on a wide range of topics, including data, design, DevOps, management, business—and much more.

Start your free trial at:
oreilly.com/safari

(No credit card required.)